T0308626

HUNTING TRAILS ON THREE CONTINENTS

GIANT SABLE ANTELOPE

As mounted for Academy of Natural Sciences of Philadelphia.

HUNTING TRAILS ON THREE CONTINENTS

Edited by
George Bird Grinnell,
Kermit Roosevelt,
W. Redmond Cross,
and Prentiss N. Gray

THE DERRYDALE PRESS
Lanham and New York

THE DERRYDALE PRESS

Published in the United States of America
by The Derrydale Press
4720 Boston Way, Lanham, Maryland 20706

Distributed by NATIONAL BOOK NETWORK, INC.

Library of Congress Cataloging-in-Publication Data
Hunting trails on three continents : the book of the Boone and Crockett Club /
edited by George Bird Grinnell ... [et al.],
    p. cm.
Originally published: New York : The Derrydale Press, c1933.
ISBN 1-58667-063-8 (cloth : alk. paper)
    1.   Hunting. 2. Natural History. I. Grinnell, George Bird, 1849-1938.

SK31 .G66 2001
799.2—dc21   00-045180

CONTENTS

CONTENTS

List of Illustrations

[v]

PREFACE

The first book of the Boone and Crockett Club was published forty years ago. The one before you is the seventh volume.

Its contents cover a wide range; there are accounts of expeditions toward the North Pole and to the south of the Equator. Some of those relating to wild animals possess peculiar interest, for they deal with species about which little has been published. Of these, "The Panda," by Kermit Roosevelt, is noteworthy.

The books of the Boone and Crockett Club, as is well known, are made up of contributions from members of the club. Readers generally will feel a sincere gratitude to those who have contributed the accounts of their experiences here published. It is hoped that these may inspire other members to set down what they have seen and done.

The Boone and Crockett Club has a unique history. It was founded at a dinner given at the home of the Hon. Theodore Roosevelt, in December, 1887. Among those present were E. P. Rogers, Archibald Rogers, J. Coleman Drayton, Thomas Paton, Col. J. E. Jones, Elliott Roosevelt, J. West Roosevelt, Theodore Roosevelt, Rutherford Stuyvesant and George Bird Grinnell. Of these men but two — J.

Coleman Drayton and George Bird Grinnell — are now living.

Founded primarily for the promotion of sport and exploration, the Boone and Crockett Club has become one of the most influential bodies in this country for the conservation and study of wild life. In a report made in 1875 to Colonel William Ludlow to accompany his *Reconnaissance from Carroll, Montana, to the Yellowstone National Park and Return*, I said: "It may not be out of place here, to call your attention to the terrible destruction of large game, for the hides alone, which is constantly going on in those portions of Montana and Wyoming through which we passed. Buffalo, elk, mule-deer and antelope are being slaughtered by thousands each year, without regard to age or sex, and at all seasons. The territories referred to have game laws, but, of course, they are imperfect, and cannot, in the present condition of the country, be enforced. Much, however, might be done to prevent the reckless destruction of the animals to which I have referred, by the officers stationed on the frontier, and a little exertion in this direction would be well repaid by the increase of large game in the vicinity of the posts where it was not unnecessarily and wantonly destroyed. Unless in some way the destruction of these animals can be checked, the large game still so abundant in some localities will ere long be exterminated."

From that time, through the medium of various periodicals, and from Washington, a bitter but successful fight has been waged to keep the Yellowstone Park from being used for commercial purposes. In 1893 I sent out the first expedition that had ever visited the Yellowstone Park in winter. This expedition led to the capture of a poacher who was killing buffalo in the Park. Reports of the conditions there were spread all over the land through the newspapers and in 1894 led to the enactment of the first laws protecting the Park game. The declaration that the sale of game should be prohibited was a novel idea and was at first received by the public with amusement, for it was not supposed that the commercial forces who were buying and selling game could be influenced by the cry, "Stop the sale of game." But we kept steadily at work and the law was passed.

As a result of the growing interest in conservation, in 1904 the Hon. George Shiras, 3d, proposed a law protecting migratory birds, and largely due to the active and enthusiastic support of this measure by the Boone and Crockett Club, in 1913 it became law.

In 1885 I first visited the country which is now known as the Glacier National Park. I continued to go there each summer and autumn for a number of years. I felt that the country was too beautiful to be given over to commercial purposes, and finally we succeeded in having the territory set aside as a national park. Since then many people have gone there to admire its beauty and to study nature.

In 1887 William Hallett Phillips of the Boone and Crockett Club succeeded in interesting Mr. Lamar, then Secretary of the Interior, and a number of congressmen in the forests, and gradually all these persons began to work together. By the close of the first Cleveland administration, while no legislation had been secured looking toward forest protection, a number of men in Washington had come to feel an interest in the subject. Finally on March 3, 1891, was passed the bill on which our national forest system is based. Later, under Roosevelt and Pinchot, the forest reserves were vastly increased. Through the efforts of Madison Grant, the great sequoias in California have been preserved. Mount McKinley, largely through the work of Charles Sheldon, was made a national park.

Through the initiative of our present president, Madison Grant, the Boone and Crockett Club was primarily responsible in bringing about the legislation which led to the formation of the New York Zoölogical Society. Madison Grant himself was executive secretary of the Society until he became its president.

Since the forming of the club we have had two dinners a year and committee meetings as occasion demanded. The club has had many distinguished visitors from this country and abroad. Through the latter, the club has been an instrument in establishing national parks and game refuges in Europe.

The work we have done in this country has been broad in its scope. The publications of the club form a valuable record of natural history, for often the writers have been naturalists and keen observers of the habits of animals and birds, giving the flora and fauna of the countries they described; and many have written in a delightful manner which makes these scientific accounts most interesting reading. These publications also afford a permanent record of the great work done by the Boone and Crockett Club in the protection of game and the conservation of natural resources, which record will become more valuable as time passes.

GEORGE BIRD GRINNELL.

New York, June, 1933.

From a painting by Carl Rungius.

ANTLERS, LIKE A GREAT BASKET, CROWN MOOSE

CHAPTER I.

The Vanished Game of Yesterday

BY MADISON GRANT

Few realize how recently the game conditions in the Atlantic States approximated those of the far West. For the present generation of big game hunters it is difficult to appreciate that there were Bison, herds of them, in Pennsylvania, Wapiti in western New York, Moose in the Adirondacks, and Caribou in Maine at no distant day.

It is high time that a definite record be made of the last occurrences of these animals east of the Alleghany Mountains. We should secure the last remaining specimens of antlers before they vanish into the attic and oblivion. There must exist in unknown localities antlers of the Adirondack Moose, which were numerous until the fifties of the last century.

We are accustomed to read about the New England Turkey used by the Puritans for Thanksgiving dinners, but that was in the distant past. The Labrador Duck and the Heath Hen were common in the days of our fathers, and the last Passenger Pigeon died in the Cincinnati Zoo on September 1, 1914.

The next generation will see these conditions duplicated in the Rockies and the Far West, and it is only in Alaska that we may be able to maintain primitive conditions approximating those of the whole country when first settled.

The original balance of life still exists to a large extent in Alaska, a situation which calls for the best efforts of big game hunters to preserve intact the immense Brown Bear, largest of carnivores, the giant Moose of the Kenai, and the huge Caribou of the Cassiar Mountains of British Columbia.

The road to ultimate extermination of all these game animals leads through an ever declining size and vigor. The Red Deer of Europe are all of one species. Today the stags of Scotland cannot compare with those of Germany, nor can the Red Deer of Germany compare with those of the Carpathians, nor can these Red Deer of the Carpathians bear comparison with those of the Caucasus. The collection of giant Red Deer antlers in the Castle of Moritzburg near Dresden, Saxony, contains huge specimens of antlers, collected three hundred years ago, which simply do not exist on living animals in Europe today. This decline in size is the result of hunting for trophies. Such hunting kills the finest bulls with the finest antlers and leaves the breeding to be done by the inferior males. The inevitable result is an ever increasing decline in the size and vigor of the stock.

The size of game animals and the massiveness of their antlers were always impressive in new countries, but the search for big trophies destroyed the huge Wapiti and Big Horn in the Rocky Mountain states.

There is need of an energetic writer to describe the condition of big mammals in Europe from the time when Caesar said that the Urus, or Wild Ox of Gaul, was as big as an elephant; and from the time when Siegfried in the Vosges Mountains hunted the Wisent and the Schelk, an animal so completely vanished that we do not know what it was. From those times down to the present such a history would run parallel to the history of what is going on in North America today.

When Europeans first reached the Atlantic Coast of America, they found there a limited number of species of animals closely analagous to those of Europe, but of even less variety of species. This American fauna, like that of the forest faunas the world over, was not numerous in individuals. It was not until the settlers reached the plains that they found huge herds of bison and antelopes, though not in anything like the abundance of the game herds of the South African veldt.

The last glaciation seems to have destroyed almost

all of the original American fauna. The animals found here by the settlers were Old World types, which had come in from Asia, for the most part over the Bering Sea land connection in post glacial times. Practically only the American Pronghorn Antelope is native to America and is a single member of a family confined to the New World.

The American White-Tailed Deer and Mule Deer (*Odocoileus*) are also native to this country, being descended from a member of the *Cervidae* with a very simple, single-beamed, unbranched antler. They developed their complex antlers in this country.

Nearly all the characteristic American animals are relatively recent arrivals from Eurasia, such as the wolf, red fox (*Vulpes*), (but not the gray fox, (*Urocyon*), beaver, otter, wolverine, marten, lynx and others.

The Mountain Sheep, of which there are several species, ranged down the Rockies into Mexico. It is closely related to the sheep of Kamchatka (*O. nivicola*). The largest of our mountain sheep were found very recently on the Brazeau River in Alberta.

There was a widely believed myth of an ibex found in the Sierras. This was probably a female mountain sheep with short straight horns, or else a domestic goat run wild which had been introduced by the Spaniards.

4

The White Mountain Goat (*Oreamnos*) is miscalled, as it is not a "goat" but a Rupicaprine or cliff-dwelling antelope. It ranges in America from the Knik River at Cook's Inlet, Alaska, where it culminates in size, down through the Canadian Rockies to the United States border, which it crosses at a few points. It thrives best in mountain ranges, where the glaciers and snow banks persist the year round. It is a slow-moving animal, ill adapted for descending to valleys for its water supply, so that it does not extend into the arid mountains of the South. It is related to the Chamois of Europe, the Serow of Japan, the Goral of China and the Takin of south eastern Asia.

BISON

The American Bison, misnamed the Buffalo, was perhaps the most typical American animal and is associated in the minds of this generation with the prairies and plains of the West. That it extended into the Atlantic states is but little known. It existed in Colonial times in the Piedmont region from Pennsylvania southward to Georgia and was found there in the hardwood forests, but never in great numbers, on the eastern side of the Appalachians. It is generally believed to have been seen by the earliest explorers nearly as far east as the District of Columbia. Its former presence is evidenced by the names Buffalo

Run, Bull Run, Bull Creek and Buffalo Lick, which are somewhat common in the Southern States.

It is hard to believe that the Bison was relatively numerous in Pennsylvania and even extended into the southwestern corner of New York State, where the name of the city of Buffalo and of Buffalo Creek indicate their former occurrence.

Most interesting is the history of the last Buffalo in Pennsylvania, which was recorded by Henry W. Shoemaker. He tells how the last herd, numbering about one hundred, was exterminated on December 31, 1799, at Middle Creek Valley, Snyder County, Pa. This herd was well known and was deliberately killed off by a group of hunters, who stampeded the animals down the valley. In their headlong flight they encountered the log cabin of one of the hunters. The cabin door being open, the leader ran in and some of the herd followed. In their terror, the Buffalo milled around in the cabin and trampled to death the wife and children of the settler.

One of the last Bison in Pennsylvania was killed by Col. John Kelly on February 19, 1801, at Buffalo Crossing, Union County, Pa. The last two of the race known in Pennsylvania were both killed in 1810; the one in Buffalo Valley, Union County and the other in the Glades of Somerset County.

In Kentucky the Buffalo were relatively numerous,

probably more so than anywhere east of the Mississippi. By 1800 all Bison east of central Kentucky were killed off.

They were never very numerous in the old Northwest Territory north of the Ohio River. By 1810 they had disappeared in the Illinois country and states east of the Mississippi.

A few stragglers lingered in Wisconsin until 1813. The last two were killed in the great Kanawah Valley about twelve miles below Charlestown, W. Va., in 1815.

Down to the eighties of the last century they inhabited the Great Plains, in herds numbering millions, as is generally known; but the end came when the building of the Union Pacific Railroad divided the herd into a northern and a southern one. Then followed a period of indiscriminate slaughter, encouraged by army officers in order to deprive the hostile plains Indians of their means of subsistence. The last herds vanished very suddenly to the dismay of the buffalo hunters, and in 1886 William T. Hornaday had great difficulty in securing a complete group for the Smithsonian Museum at Washington. These last stragglers were killed near Big Porcupine Creek in Montana.

Twenty years later there were no wild herds, except a small band in the Yellowstone Park and a larger

7

band north of the Athabasca River in western Canada. Both these surviving bands were considered to be separate sub-species. There were several herds in private ownership, and it is from these that the existing Bison are descended. It is probable that less than one hundred animals from these domesticated herds are the ancestors of the 18,500 animals now living.

The recovery of the Bison is largely due to the foresight and energy of Dr. W. T. Hornaday, who engineered the movement for their restoration. Some of the first animals were supplied from the captive herds of the Zoological Park, New York City. This is the most dramatic incident of the restoration of a vanishing species in America, and is an example of what can be done with other large mammals.

Our American Bison is closely related to the European Wisent, which is generally miscalled the Aurochs. Since the World War this fine animal has been reduced to the verge of extinction. In 1930 there were known to be living only 59 specimens, of which 32 were females. The New York Zoological Society at that time took an active interest in the attempted restoration of this European species and sent Dr. W. Reid Blair abroad on its behalf to help organize the rescue work undertaken by the International Society for the Preservation of the Wisent. The results of the

Society's efforts have been most encouraging, although greatly hampered by international rivalries.

At present there is every reason to hope that the European Wisent, like its American cousin, will be restored and not follow the European Wild Ox, the Urus, into the limbo of forgotten and almost legendary large mammals.

WAPITI

Next to the Bison the most important game animal in North America was perhaps the Wapiti, miscalled the Elk.

The English-speaking settlers on their arrival knew only a limited number of names for mammals, birds and fish. As a result they applied many names erroneously to the animals they found here, often using the same names for different animals in various sections of the country.

In the case of the Wapiti, the application of the name Elk to our great deer was particularly unfortunate. As a result of this use of the name Elk, many thousands have been slaughtered for their canine teeth, which are used as a symbol of membership in the Order of Elks. These so-called tusks or "tushes" have a real money value. In this case the misuse of name has been a veritable tragedy. The true Elk or

Moose have no tooth corresponding to the prominent blunt canine of the Wapiti.

In Canada the Wapiti is sometimes called the Round Horn Elk in contrast to the Moose known as the Flat Horn Elk. While it is closely related to several forms of *Cervus* found in the mountains of northeastern Asia, it is not very close to the European Stag or Red Deer.

The primitive range of the Wapiti in the East is somewhat hard to determine, but it probably extended to the Saguenay region of Quebec. They occurred very likely in the mountainous region of western New England, but not in Maine. They were found in numbers along the eastern slope of the Appalachians, southward to northern Georgia, but were not found in the coniferous region along the Coast.

This eastern Wapiti was very likely a different species from the typical animal of the western plains, but we have very few antlers on which to base such a decision. A few are known to have been killed in New York State. Several sets of antlers are in the possession of the family of the late W. Austin Wadsworth, a former President of The Boone and Crockett Club. These animals were killed over a century ago within forty miles of Geneseo, N. Y.

Wapiti were numerous in New York State at the beginning of the nineteenth century in the southwestern counties. We have no record of their final disappearance, but a Wapiti was killed in 1834 at Bolivar, Alleghany County, N. Y.

There is no evidence of them in the Adirondacks.

There is little or nothing to show their presence in New England, although E. W. Nelson says that they were found originally in central Massachusetts.

As to their recent extension in Canada, as late as 1895 the Game Commissioner of Quebec told the writer that there were Wapiti at Grand Lake Victoria at the headwaters of the Ottawa River in Quebec. No confirmation of this has been received.

In Pennsylvania the Wapiti lingered long, and one of the last individuals, known as the "Flag Swamp Elk," was killed in Elk County, near Bradford, Penn., in 1867.

A bull and a cow are said to have been seen in Clinton County in 1868 and 1869, and a calf Elk was shot in 1877 in Decker Valley, Centre County, indicating that Elk still existed in Pennsylvania up to that date.

They were numerous in Colonial times in Kentucky and Tennessee but were destroyed there early in the nineteenth century.

In closing, a reference should be made to the name Wapiti, which has been widely and wisely applied to this great deer. As a matter of fact, the name "Waputek" is applied to the White Mountain Goat in the language of the Stony Indians in Alberta, a branch of the Blackfoot, and the name may very well have been adopted further East for the large animal of those regions, or vice-versa.

CARIBOU

Like the name of the Moose, the word Caribou is of Algonquin origin and is used to distinguish the American forms of *Rangifer* from the so-called Reindeer of Europe. It was another of the Old World mammals to enter America through the Bering Sea land connection in post glacial times. It extends over the Canadian boundary into the United States at a few points on the north, notably in the Rockies, in Minnesota and in northeastern New England.

The Caribou are divided into Barren Ground and Woodland groups. The former culminate in the Grant Caribou of the Alaska Peninsula and the latter in the Caribou of Newfoundland and the Osborn Caribou of the Cassiar Mountains.

The writer has no reason to believe that Caribou ever existed in the Adirondacks.

The Caribou, a generation ago, was abundant in the Maritime Provinces and in Maine. As they are very intolerant of human intrusion they disappeared suddenly from Maine. The last record of which the

From a painting by Carl Rungius.

THE VAST HERDS OF CARIBOU ARE DISAPPEARING

writer has personal knowledge was in 1892, when he saw a hunter with a handsome fresh Caribou head in his canoe near Sourdnahunk Lake, immediately north of Mt. Katahdin. They originally extended throughout Maine and have been known as far south as Mt. Desert Island.

Five Caribou have recently reappeared at Red Lake, Minnesota. The district has wisely been made a sanctuary known as the Red Lake Game Preserve and every protection is afforded them in the hope of their reestablishment.

MOOSE

The name of the Moose is of Algonquin origin, meaning a deer that browses.

References have been made as to its relationship to Elk or Alces, still inhabiting Scandinavia. It was to be found in the Vosges Mountains in the time of Caesar and even of Siegfried in the 5th Century. Closely related species range across Siberia. Like many of the large animals of America, they have apparently entered the continent in relatively recent times and spread from Alaska and western Canada eastward to Quebec, but were too late to enter Newfoundland or even Labrador.

In the Maritime Provinces they still occupy New Brunswick and Nova Scotia, and are numerous in

Maine. They cross the American boundary from
Manitoba into Minnesota and extend down the
Rockies as far as the Yellowstone Park. As every
hunter knows, they culminate in the giant species
found in the Kenai Peninsula.

Moose were very abundant in the Adirondacks until
about 1850. During the 50's one or two moose were
killed each year, and the last one, a female, was
killed on the eastern end of Raquette Lake in 1863.
Since then several attempts have been made, as yet
unsuccessfully, to reintroduce the Moose.

The disappearance of Moose in the Adirondacks in
the 1890's was said to have been caused by a migra-
tion northward to the Muskoka country in western
Ontario. This does not seem probable as the Moose
in Maine have shown great adaptability in adjusting
themselves to the neighborhood of man. The Moose
are unlike the Caribou in this respect. They are,
nevertheless, a migratory animal, shifting their range
through the years. Moose are said to have been found
in the Catskills, but the writer can find no satisfactory
evidence of their actual occurrence there. They probably extended south as far as the Berkshire hills in
northwestern Massachusetts.

In the early 1890's Moose were not present in the
northern part of Lake Kippewa in western Quebec,

but in later years they pushed north over the Height of Land in Quebec toward Hudson's Bay.

In the late 1890's, A. J. Stone found an Indian whose grandfather was said to be the first man of his tribe to discover Moose west of the Mackenzie River in Alberta. At this very point, in the quadrangle between the Mackenzie River, the Rocky Mountains and the Liard and Peace Rivers, is now the greatest Moose range in the world. About 1840 Moose apparently were unknown there when the grandfather of this Indian killed a huge black deer with long gray legs and flat antlers and the neighboring tribes gathered from every side to inspect this strange animal.

In parts of Canada the Moose is called the Flat Horned Elk. Forty years ago in the Ottawa country hunters recognized two types of Moose, — a short-legged variety called the Swamp Moose, and the long-legged common type known as the Ranger Moose.

VIRGINIA DEER

There is little that is new to be said about the Virginia or White-Tailed Deer, which was abundant along the Atlantic Coast, extending westward to the Pacific, where it was replaced by related species.

It was, more than any other game animal, the food of the pioneers. In most parts of its range it has held its own against advancing civilization and has shown a remarkable ability to adapt itself to living in the neighborhood of man. In the past, its range varied with the abundance of wolves, which were its natural enemies.

With a little reasonable protection it can be maintained indefinitely in its present numbers, although systematic hunting for the best heads may cause a decline in size and complexity of antlers.

Forty years ago in the Adirondacks a rare variety of this deer known as the "Meadow Buck" was recognized by its elaborate horns, sometimes with a forked tine, and by the retention, late into the autumn, around the base of the antlers, of the summer red coat. It was characterized by relatively short legs and was a highly prized type.

PUMA

There were only two big felines indigenous to the New World, the Jaguar and the Puma. The former entered the United States only along the southern border and in this article can be disregarded.

The Puma had a much wider range, extending from the southernmost part of South America through Mexico and the United States to southern Canada. It is still numerous in Vancouver Island, British Columbia, but did not reach Newfoundland, the Maritime Provinces, or Eastern Quebec.

In New England the eastern limit appears to have been about the Connecticut River, and there is no record of its occurrence in Maine. In the middle states it was well known and made a great impression on the frontiersmen, although there is no reason to consider it dangerous to man.

It is now practically extinct east of the Rocky Mountains, although it was numerous along the Appalachians and in West Virginia half a century ago. In 1920 there were said to be some still living in southern Florida, in southern Louisiana and in Texas.

Before describing its last stand in the East, it will be interesting to note the various names conferred on *Felis concolor*. In New England it went by the name of Catamount, but in New York and in the middle and southern states it was the Panther or "Painter," while in the Rockies it goes by the grandiose name of Mountain Lion. In Central and South America Cougar or Onca parda or Puma is used.

In Colonial times Pumas were numerous in the Catskills in New York, and they persisted in the Adirondacks as their last stronghold almost down to today. Two of the last authentic records there, were in 1888 and 1890, but there is evidence of its occurrence later. In the Game Warden's office at Albany there is a mounted specimen killed by Verplanck Colvin on Sumner Stream, February 15, 1897, and

17

the last bounty was paid for a Panther which was killed December 27, 1899. In the last week of August, 1903, a Panther was said to have been seen at Big Moose, N. Y.

H. W. Shoemaker gives records for 1911, 1913 and as late as 1922. It is obvious that these were the last known specimens to be recorded. However authentic these last dates are, it is more than probable that the Panther persisted in Pennsylvania and in New York into the present century.

They were quite numerous in Pennsylvania, forty-one being killed in a single side hunt, in which, incidentally, a hundred and nine wolves were also killed. This was, however, about 1760.

In this connection it is interesting to note that wolves, which have long since disappeared in the Adirondacks, were exterminated in Pennsylvania about 1903, although one was seen in 1916 in Clinton County, Penn.

BEARS

The Spectacled Bear of South America — Tremarctos — represents perhaps the earliest form of Bear which came to this continent from the Old World. It passed into the South American Andes over one of the early land connections and became isolated there while the parent forms in North America died out. Curiously enough, the Bear skulls found in the asphalt pits of Rancho La Brea on the outskirts of Los Angeles, California belong to this type (*Arctotherium*).

The next Bear to arrive over the land connections with Asia was apparently the Black Bear group (*Euarctos*) now represented in North America from Mexico northward by several slightly divergent forms.

The third group to arrive from Asia, which was much more closely related to the Old World forms, was the Grizzly (*Ursus horribilis*). It did not cross the Mississippi, but is represented on the Barren Ground of Canada by the Barren Ground Grizzly (*Ursus richardsoni*). This Barren Ground Grizzly was supposed to have disappeared but was rediscovered some twenty years ago on the Barren Grounds. There is strong evidence of the existence of a new species of Bear, possibly Grizzly, in the north of Labrador near Ungava, and recent confirmation of its occurrence has just been received.

The California Grizzly (*U. Magister*), well known to the Forty-Niners, has become entirely extinct within in a generation and the typical Grizzly has disappeared from the Plains region.

In Colonial times, the only Bear known to the settlers was the Black Bear and some of them had a bad

reputation and were called Sinika (Seneca) Bears.
The most curious thing about the Black Bear is a color
variation which is found only in such portions of its
range as are occupied also by the Grizzly. This brown
or cinnamon phase is found in the same litter as the
black cubs but is said to be larger and more savage.
As a result, hunters in the far West considered the
cinnamon Bear a cross-breed between a Black Bear
mother and a Grizzly father.

Two other color phases of the Black Bear are found
in the Northwest. They are both extremely rare. One
is a blue color phase known as the Glacier Bear
(*Ursus emmonsi*) found near Yakutat Bay, Alaska.
The other is Kermode's Bear (*U. kermodei*) which
is found at Gribble Island off the British Columbia
coast and is of an almost pure white color.

The Brown Bears of Alaska, representing several
different species, were not known until the 1890's
and were first called "Fish Bear" from their salmon-
eating habits and from their resemblance to the
Kamchatka Fish Bear (*Ursus piscator*) to which they
are closely related. It is the largest living carnivore
and deserves thorough protection.

These Brown Bears occupy the coastal regions of
Alaska, and were undoubtedly the last group to arrive
from Asia.

The Polar Bear (*Thalarctos*) is of circumpolar distribution. It is abundant and formerly bred freely on the islands of the Bering Sea, especially Hall Island. This island, in the northern part of the Bering Sea near the Alaskan coast, has been celebrated for its Polar Bears. Being always frozen in the solid winter ice of Bering Sea, a new supply of Bears from the North is received each year. When left there after the ice recedes they find abundant food in berries. Hall Island should be made a sanctuary, both for white Bears and Walrus, as it is entirely treeless and uninhabited.

In closing, it may be remarked that the Cave Bear (*Ursus Spaeleus*) of Europe, which was hunted by Paleolithic Man, had the same curious habit of stretching to its utmost height and scratching with its claws on the walls of the caves precisely as all American Bears, Grizzly or Black, scratch on "bear trees". The purpose of this is probably to sharpen their claws just as a cat sharpens its claws on the parlor furniture.

In conclusion, it should be pointed out that the range of the Grizzly has been so restricted in the United States that this Bear verges on extinction. In fact, outside of national parks, such as the Yellowstone, it is almost extinct. It has almost vanished. Ten years ago, in Colorado, where this Bear was very numerous two generations ago, the writer was told that there were only three wild specimens living in the state.

The Black Bear has shown great ability to adjust itself to the presence of man and still holds its own in places like Florida, Maine, the Adirondacks and in the Pocono Mountains in northeastern Pennsylvania. It is a harmless and interesting animal and if given half a chance can last on indefinitely.

CHAPTER II.

An Epic of the Polar Air Lanes*

By LINCOLN ELLSWORTH

"Life is a ball in the hands of chance."

May 21st was the day we had long awaited, when, with our two Dornier-Wal flying boats we were ready to take off from the ice at King's Bay and start into the Unknown. We were carrying seventy-eight hundred pounds above the estimated maximum lift. We were compelled to leave behind our radio equipment, which would mean an additional three hundred pounds. Our provisions were sufficient to last one month, at the rate of two pounds per day per man. The daily ration list per man was:

Pemmican	400 gr.
Milk Chocolate	250 "
Oatmeal Biscuits	125 "
Powered Milk	100 "
Malted Milk Tablets.........	125 "

At 4:15 P.M. all was ready for the start. The 450 H.P. Rolls-Royce motors were turned over for warming up. At five o'clock the full horse power was

* Lincoln Ellsworth's account from "Our Polar Flight."

23

turned on. We moved. The N. 25 had Captain Amundsen as navigator. Riiser-Larsen was his pilot, and Feucht mechanic. I was navigator of N. 24 with Dietrichson for pilot, and Omdal was my mechanic; six men in all.

During the first two hours of our flight, after leaving Amsterdam Islands, we ran into a heavy bank of fog and rose one thousand meters to clear it. This ascent was glorified by as beautiful a natural phenomenon as I have ever seen. Looking down into the mist, we saw a double halo in the middle of which the sun cast a perfect shadow of our plane. Evanescent and phantom-like, these two multicolored halos beckoned us enticingly into the Unknown. I recalled the ancient legend which says that the rainbow is a token that man shall not perish by water. The fog lasted until midway between latitudes eighty-two and eighty-three. Through rifts in the mist we caught glimpses of the open sea. This lasted for an hour; then, after another hour, the ocean showed, strewn with small ice floes, which indicated the fringe of the Polar pack. Then, to quote Captain Amundsen, "suddenly the mist disappeared and the entire panorama of Polar ice stretched away before our eyes — the most spectacular sheet of snow and ice ever seen by man from an aerial perspective." From our altitude we could overlook sixty or seventy miles in any direction. The far-flung expanse was strikingly beautiful in its simplicity. There was nothing to break the even monotony of snow and ice except a network of narrow cracks, or "leads," which scarred this white surface and was the only indication to an aerial observer of the ceaseless movement of the Polar pack. We had crossed the threshold into the Unknown! I was thrilled at the thought that never before had man lost himself with such speed — seventy-five miles per hour — into unknown space. Now, for the first time, the silence of ages was being broken by the roar of our motors.

We were but gnats in an immense void. We had lost all contact with civilization. Time and distance suddenly seemed to count for nothing. What lay ahead was all that mattered now.

> *"Something hidden. Go and find it.*
> *Go and look behind the Ranges —*
> *Something lost behind the Ranges,*
> *Lost and waiting for you. Go!"*

On we sped for eight hours, till the sun had shifted from the west to a point directly ahead of us. By all rights we should now be at the Pole, for our dead reckoning showed that we had traveled just one thousand kilometers (six hundred miles), at seventy-five miles per hour, but shortly after leaving Amsterdam Islands we had run into a heavy north-east wind, which had been steadily driving us westward. Our fuel supply was now about half exhausted, and at this juncture, strangely enough, just ahead of us, was the first open lead of water large enough for an aeroplane to land in, that we had encountered on our whole journey north. There was nothing left now but to descend for observation, to learn where we were. As Captain Amundsen's plane started to circle for a landing, his rear motor backfired and stopped, so that he finally disappeared among a lot of ice hummocks with only one motor going.

This was at 1 A.M. on the morning of May 22nd. The lead ran east and west, meeting our course at right angles. It was an awful looking hole. We circled for about ten minutes, looking for enough open water to land in. The lead was choked up with a chaotic mass of floating ice floes, and it looked as if some one had started to dynamite the ice pack. Ice blocks standing on edge or piled high on top of one another, hummocks and pressure-ridges, were all that greeted our eyes. It was like trying to land in the Grand Canyon.

We came down in a little lagoon among the ice-floes, and as the plane's momentum carried us over towards a huge drifting ice-cake, Dietrichson commenced madly pulling a bell-cord which connected from the pilot's seat with the tail of the plane, and yelling "Omdal, Omdal, the plane's leaking like hell!" and so it was. Anchoring our plane to the huge ice-cake, we jumped out with our sextant and artificial horizon to find out where we were. Not knowing what to expect, I carried my rifle, but after our long flight I was a bit unsteady on my legs, tumbling down into the deep snow, and choking up the barrel. Our eyes were bloodshot and we were almost stone-deaf after listening to the unceasing roar of our motors for eight hours; the stillness seemed intensified.

Looking around on landing, I had the feeling that nothing but death could be at home in this part of the world, and that there could not possibly be any life in such an environment, when I was surprised to see a seal pop up his head beside the plane. I am sure he was as surprised as we were, for he raised himself out of the water to inspect us and seemed not at all afraid to approach, as he came almost up to us. We had no thought of taking his life, for we expected to be off and on our way again towards the Pole after our observation. His curiosity satisfied, he disappeared, and, during our entire stay in the ice, we never saw another sign of life in those waters.

Our observations showed that we had come down in Lat. 87° 44′ N., Long. 10° 20′ West. As our flight

meridian was 12° East, where we landed was, therefore, 22° 20′ off our course. This westerly drift had
cost us nearly a degree in latitude and enough extra
fuel to have carried us to the Pole. As it was, we were
just one hundred and thirty-six nautical miles from
it. At the altitude at which we had been flying just
before descending, our visible horizon was forty-six
miles; which means that we had been able to see
ahead as far as Lat. 88° 30′ N. or to within just ninety
miles of the North Pole. We had left civilization, and
eight hours later we were able to view the earth
within ninety miles of the goal that it had taken Peary
twenty-three years to reach. Truly "the efforts of one
generation may become the commonplace of the next."

When we had finished taking our observation, we
began to wonder where N. 25 was. We crawled up
on all the high hummocks nearby and with our field-
glasses searched the horizon. Dietrichson remarked
that perhaps Amundsen had gone on to the Pole. "It
would be just like him," he said. It was not until noon,
however, of the 22nd that we spotted them from an
especially high hill of ice. The N. 25 lay with her
nose pointing into the air at an angle of forty-five
degrees, among a lot of rough hummocks and against
a huge cake of old blue Arctic ice about forty feet
thick, three miles away. It was a rough-looking country, and the position of the N. 25 was terrible to

behold. To us it looked as though she had crashed into this ice.

We of the N. 24 were not in too good shape, where we were. We had torn the nails loose on the bottom of our plane, when we took off from King's Bay, so that she was leaking badly; in fact, the water was now above the bottom of the petrol tanks. Also, our forward motor was disabled. In short, we were badly wrecked. Things looked so hopeless to us at that moment that it seemed as though the impossible would have to happen ever to get us out. No words so well express our mental attitude at that time as these lines of Swinburne's:

"From hopes cut down across a world of fears,
We gaze with eyes too passionate for tears,
Where Faith abides, though Hope be put to flight."

That first day, while Dietrichson and I had tried to reach the N. 25, Omdal had been trying to repair the motor. We dragged our canvas canoe up over hummocks and tumbled into ice crevasses until we were thoroughly exhausted. The snow was two to three feet deep all over the ice, and we floundered through it, never knowing what we were going to step on next. Twice Dietrichson went down between the floes and only by hanging onto the canoe was he able to save

himself from sinking. After half a mile of this we
were forced to give up and return.

We pitched our tent on top of the ice floe, moved
all our equipment out of the plane into it, and tried
to make ourselves as comfortable as possible. But
there was no sleep for us and very little rest during
the next five days. Omdal was continually working on
the motor, while Dietrichson and I took turns at the
pump. Only by the most incessant pumping were we
able to keep the water down below the gasoline tanks.

Although we had located the N. 25, they did not
see us till the afternoon of the second day, which was
May 23rd. We had taken the small inflated balloons,
which the meteorologist had given us with which to
obtain data regarding the upper air strata, and after
tying pieces of flannel to them set them loose. We
hoped that the wind would drift them over to N. 25
and so indicate to them in which direction to look for
us. But the wind blew them in the wrong direction,
or else they drifted too low and got tangled up in the
rough ice.

Through all that first day the wind was blowing
from the north and we could see a few patches of
open water. On the second day the wind shifted to
the south and the ice began to draw in on us. It was
as though we were in the grasp of a gigantic hand

that was slowly but surely closing. We had a feeling that soon we would be crushed.

On the third day, May 24th, the temperature was — 11.5 c., and we had trouble with our pump freezing. The two planes were now slowly drifting together, and we established a line of communication, so that we knew each other's positions pretty well. Semaphoring is tedious work, for it requires two men; one with the flag, and the other with a pair of field-glasses to read the signals. It took us a whole hour merely to signal our positions, after which we must wait for their return signals and then reply to them.

On this day, after an exchange of signals, we decided to try to reach Amundsen. We packed our canvas canoe, put it on our sledge, and started across what looked to us like mountainous hummocks. After only going a few hundred yards we had to give up. The labor was too exhausting. With no sleep for three days, and only liquid food, our strength was not what it should have been. Leaving our canvas canoe, we now made up our packs of fifty pounds each, and pushed on. We did not know whether we should, or should not return to our plane again.

According to my diary we traveled the first two miles in two hours and fifteen minutes, when we came upon a large lead that separated us from the N. 25 and which we could find no way to cross. We talked to them by signal and they advised our returning. So, after a seven-hour trip, we returned to our sinking plane, having covered perhaps five and one half miles in about the same length of time it had taken us to fly from Spitzbergen to Lat. 87° 44'. Arriving at our plane, we pitched camp again and cooked a heavy pemmican soup over our Primus stove. Dietrichson gave us a surprise by producing a small tin of George Washington coffee. We took some of the pure alcohol carried for the Primus stove and put in into the coffee, and with pipes lighted felt more or less happy.

As we smoked in silence, each with his own thoughts, Dietrichson suddenly clasped his hands to his eyes, exclaiming: "Something is the matter with my eyes!" He was snow blind, but never having experienced this before, did not know what had happened to him. We had been careful to wear our snow-glasses during most of the journey, but perhaps not quite careful enough. After bandaging Dietrichson's eyes, Omdal and I put him to bed and then continued with our smoking and thoughts. It seems strange, when I think back now, that during those days nothing that happened greatly surprised us. Everything that occurred was accepted as part of the day's work. This is an interesting sidelight on man's adaptability to his environment.

All our energies were now being bent in getting

the N. 24 up on the ice floe, for if we left her in the lead, we knew she would be crushed. The whole cake we were on was only about two hundred meters in diameter, and there was only one level stretch on it of eighty meters. It was laborious work for Dietrichson and myself to try to clear away the soggy wet snow, for all we had to work with was one clumsy homemade wooden shovel and our ice-anchor. As I would loosen the snow by picking at it with the anchor, Dietrichson would shovel it away.

Looking through our glasses at N. 25, we could see the propellers going, and Amundsen pulling up and down on the wings, trying to loosen the plane from the ice, but she did not budge. On the morning of May 26th, Amundsen signaled to us, asking that if we couldn't save our plane to come over and help them. We had so far succeeded in getting the nose of our plane up onto the ice-cake, but with only one engine working it was impossible to do more. Anyway, she was safe now from sinking, but not from being crushed, should the ice press in on her. During the five days of our separation the ice had so shifted that the two planes were now plainly in sight of each other and only half a mile apart. During all that time the ice had been in continual movement, so that now all the heavy ice had moved out from between the two camps. We signaled to the N. 25 that we were com-

33

ing, and making up loads of eighty pounds per man, we started across the freshly frozen lead that separated us from our companions. We were well aware of the chances we were taking, crossing this new ice, but we saw no other alternative. We must get over to N. 25 with all possible speed if we were ever to get back again to civilization.

With our feet shoved loosely into our skis, for we never fastened them on here for fear of getting tangled up, should we fall into the sea, we shuffled along, slowly feeling our way over the thin ice. Omdal was in the lead, myself and Dietrichson — who had recovered from his slight attack of snow-blindness the next day — following in that order. Suddenly I heard Dietrichson yelling behind me, and before I knew what it was all about Omdal ahead of me cried out also and disappeared as though the ice beneath him had suddenly opened and swallowed him. The ice under me started to sag, and I quickly jumped sideways to avoid the same fate that had overtaken my companions. There just happened to be some old ice beside me and that was what saved me. Lying down on my stomach, partly on this ledge of old ice, and partly out on the new ice, I reached the skis out and pulled Dietrichson over to where I could grab his pack and partly pull him out onto the firmer ice, where he lay panting and exhausted. Then I turned my attention to Omdal. Only his pallid face showed above the water. It is strange, when I think that both these Norwegians had been conversing almost wholly in their native tongue, that Omdal was now crying in English, "I'm gone! I'm gone!" — and he was almost gone too. The only thing that kept him from going way under was the fact that he kept digging his fingers into the ice. I reached him just before he sank and held him by his pack until Dietrichson could crawl over to me and hold him up, while I cut off the pack. It took all the remaining strength of the two of us to drag Omdal up onto the old ice. It was not until three years after, when, in 1927, Omdal came to America that he showed me five teeth which he had completely broken off, while vainly trying to hang on the ice edge and my extended ski. This was shortly before Omdal was engaged to pilot Mrs. Grayson's ill-fated "Dawn" in which he lost his life.

Our companions could not reach us, neither could they see us, as a few old ice hummocks of great size stood directly in front of N. 25. They could do nothing but listen to the agonizing cries of their fellowmen in distress. We finally succeeded in getting over to our companions, who gave us dry clothes and hot chocolate, and we were soon all right again, except for Omdal's swollen and lacerated hands. Both men had lost their skis. In view of the probability of being forced to tramp to Greenland, four hundred miles away, the loss of these skis seemed a terrible calamity.

I was surprised at the change only five days had wrought in Captain Amundsen. He seemed to me to have aged ten years. We now joined with our companions in the work of freeing the N. 25 from her precarious position. As stated before, when Captain Amundsen's plane had started to come down into the lead, his rear motor back-fired, and he was forced to land with only one motor working, which accounted for the position in which we now found N. 25. She lay half on and half off an ice floe; her nose was up on the cake and her tail down in the sea. Coming down thus had reduced her speed and saved her from crashing into the cake of old blue ice, which was directly ahead. It seemed amazing that whereas five days ago the N. 25 had found enough open water to land in, now there was not enough to be seen anywhere sufficient to launch a rowboat in. She was tightly locked in the grip of the shifting ice.

A most orderly routine was being enforced at Amundsen's camp. Regular hours for everything — to work, sleep, eat, smoke and talk; no need to warn these men, as so many explorers had been compelled to do, not to give one another the story of their lives,

36

lest boredom come. The Norwegians have their long periods of silence in which the glance of an eye or the movement of a hand takes the place of conversation. This, no doubt, accounts for the wonderful harmony that existed during the whole twenty-five days of our imprisonment in the ice. One might expect confusion and disorganization under the conditions confronting us. But it was just the reverse. We did everything as if we had oceans of time in which to do it. It was this calm, cool, and unhurried way of doing things which kept our spirits up and eventually got us out of a desperate situation. No one ever got depressed or blue, although we did find Feucht pretty blue one day when we returned to camp to see him perched on top of the gasoline tank, dejectedly holding both jaws in his hands, after vainly having tried to extract an aching molar with a monkey wrench. His sufferings now were greater than before.

We elected Omdal our cook. Although we felt better nourished and stronger after our noon cup of pemmican broth, it was always our morning and evening cup of chocolate that we most looked forward to. How warming and cheering that hot draught was! Captain Amundsen remarked that the only time we were happy up there was when either the hot chocolate was going down our throats, or else when we were rolled up in our reindeer sleeping bags. The rest of the time we were more or less miserable, but never do I remember a time when we lost faith. The after-compartment of our plane — a dismal hole — served as kitchen, dining-room and sleeping-quarters, but it was draughty and uncomfortable, and it seemed always a relief after our meals to get out again into the open. The cold duralumin metal overhead was coated with hoarfrost which turned into a steady drip as the heat from our little Primus stove, together with that from our steaming chocolate, started to warm up the cabin. Feucht always sat opposite me — I say sat, but he squatted — we all squatted on the bottom of the plane with our chocolate on our knees. I remember how I used covertly to watch him eating his three oatmeal wafers and drinking his chocolate. I always tried to hold mine back so as not to finish before him. I had the strange illusion that if I finished first it was because he was getting more to eat than I. I particularly recall one occasion, two weeks later, after we had cut our rations in half, when I purposely hid my last biscuit in the folds of my parka, and the satisfaction it gave me to draw it out and eat it after Feucht had laid his cup aside. It was a stirring of one of those primitive instincts which, hidden beneath the veneer of our civilization, lie ever ready to assert themselves upon reversion to primitive conditions. We smoked a pipe apiece of tobacco after each meal, but unfortunately we had taken only a few days' supply of smoking stuff. When that went, we had to resort to Riiser-Larsen's private stock of rank, black chewing twist. It took a real hero to smoke that tobacco after moistening it so as to make it burn slower and thus hold out longer. It always gave us violent hiccoughs.

We were compelled to give up our civilized habits of washing or changing our clothes. It was too cold to undress, and we could not spare the fuel to heat any water after our necessary cooking was done.

During all our stay in the ice I never saw Captain Amundsen take a drink of water. I was always thirsty after the pemmican, and when I called for water, he said he could not understand how I could drink so much water.

Captain Amundsen and I slept together in the pilot's cockpit, which we covered over with canvas to darken it at night. I was never able to get used to the monotony of continuous daylight and found it very wearing. With the exception of Riiser-Larsen the rest of the men slept on their skis stretched across the rear-compartment to keep them off the metal bottom. Riiser-Larsen had all to himself the tail, into which he was compelled to crawl on hands and knees.

It took us a whole day to construct a slip and work our plane up onto the ice-cake. On our slim rations, the work was exhausting and, besides, we had only the crudest of implements with which to work; three wooden shovels, a two-pound pocket safety-ax, and an ice anchor. Through hopeless necessity we slashed at the ice. When one considers our scant diet, it is remarkable, what work we accomplished with these implements! Captain Amundsen conservatively estimates that we moved three hundred tons of ice during the twenty-five days of our imprisonment up there in order to free our plane.

The floe we were on measured three hundred meters in diameter, but we needed a four hundred-meter course from which to take off. Our best chance, of course, would be to take off in open water, but the wind continued to blow from the south, and the south wind did not make for open water.

Riiser-Larsen was tireless in his search for an ice floe of the right dimensions. While the rest of us were relaxing, he was generally to be seen on the skyline searching with that tireless energy that was so characteristic of him. Silent and resourceful, he was the rock on which we were building our hopes.

The incessant toil went on. On May 28th the N. 25 was safe from the screwing of the pack-ice. On this day we took soundings, which gave us a depth of the Polar Sea of three thousand, seven hundred and fifty meters (12,375 feet). This depth corresponds almost exactly to the altitude of Mont Blanc above the village of Chamounix. Up to this time our only thought had been to free the plane and continue on to the Pole, but now, facing the facts as they confronted us, it seemed inadvisable to consider anything else but a return to Spitzbergen. The thermometer during these days registered between —9°c. and —11°c.

On May 29th Dietrichson, Omdal and I, by a circuitous route, were able to reach the N. 24 with our canvas canoe and sled. We must get the remaining gasoline and provisions. Our only hope of reaching Spitzbergen lay in salvaging this fuel from the N. 24. We cut out one of the empty tanks, filled it from one of the fresh ones, loaded it in our canoe, put the canoe on the sled and started back. And now we found that a large lead had opened up behind us, over which we were barely able to get across ourselves, so we had to leave the tank and supplies on the further side over night. The next day the lead had closed again and Dietrichson and Omdal succeeded in getting the gasoline over. The light sled got slightly broken among the rough hummocks, which was an additional catastrophe, in view of the probability of having to walk to Greenland.

We now had two hundred and forty-five liters additional fuel — fifteen hundred liters altogether — or a margin of three hundred liters on which to make

Spitzbergen, provided we could get off immediately.

On May 31st an inventory of our provisions showed that we had on hand:

285 half-pound cakes of pemmican,

300 cakes of chocolate,

   3 ordinary cracker-tins of oatmeal biscuits,

   3 20-lb. sacks of powdered milk,

   3 sausages, 12-lbs. each,

 42 condensed milk tins of Horlick's Malted Milk Tablets,

 25 liters of kerosene for our Primus stove (we later used motor fuel for cooking).

Our observations for latitude and longitude this day showed our position to be 87.32 N. and 7.30 W. It meant that the whole pack had been steadily drifting southeast since our arrival. It was at least some consolation to know that we were slowly but surely drifting south, where we knew there was game. How we should have liked to have had that seal we saw the first day! We had seen no life of any description since, neither in the water nor in the air, not even a track on the snow to show that there was another living thing in these latitudes but ourselves. It is a land of misery and death.

With a view to working the longest possible time in an attempt to get the N. 25 clear, and at the same time have sufficient provisions left with which to reach

Greenland, Captain Amundsen felt that it was necessary to cut down our daily rations to three hundred grams per man, or just one half pound per man per day. This amounted to one-half the ration that Peary fed his dogs a day on his journey to the Pole. By thus reducing our rations, he figured that our provisions would last for two months longer.

Captain Amundsen now set June 15th as the date upon which a definite decision must be arrived at. On that date something must be done; so a vote was taken, each man having the option of either starting on foot for Greenland on that date, or else sticking by the plane with the hope of open water coming while watching the food dwindle. There was much divided opinion. It seemed absurd to consider starting out on a long tramp when right by our side was six hundred and forty horse power lying idle, which could take us back to civilization within eight hours. Captain Amundson was for staying by the plane. He said that with the coming of summer the leads would open. Riiser-Larsen said he would start walking on June 15th. Feucht said he would not walk a foot and that he would stick by the motors. Omdal said he would do what the majority did, and I said I would prefer to wait until June 14th before making a decision.

My own mind was pretty well made up that if I

ever succeeded in traveling one hundred miles towards Greenland on foot, I would be doing well. Yet sitting down by the plane and watching the last of the food go was a thing that ran counter to my every impulse. I agreed with Captain Amundsen that I should much prefer to "finish it" on my feet. I think that all really believed that in our worn-out condition carrying thirty pounds on our backs and dragging a canvas canoe along with which to cross open leads, none of us would be able to reach the Greenland coast.

Most of our doubt regarding the tramp to Greenland, of course, came from our not knowing just how far the bad country that we were in extended. Climb up as high as we could, we were never able to see the end of it. Whether it extended to Greenland or not was the question, and that made it hard for us to decide what course to take.

After our evening cup of chocolate Captain Amundsen and I generally would put on our skis and take a few turns around the ice floe we were on before turning into our sleeping-bags. I usually asked him on these occasions what he thought of the situation. His reply was that things looked pretty bad, but he was quick to add that it had always been his experience in life that when things were blackest, there was generally light ahead.

On May 31st there was eight inches of ice in the

lead on the far side of the floe we were on. We decided to try a take-off on this new ice. From our ice-cake down into the lead there was a six-foot drop, so that it was necessary to construct a slip upon which to get our plane down into the lead. We built this slip in accordance with standard road-making principles—first heavy blocks of ice, then filling in on top with smaller pieces, and then tiny lumps and loose snow, on top of which we spread a layer of loose snow which froze into a smooth surface. It took us two days to build this slip and to level off the ice ahead for five hundred meters.

At this time we had established regular nightly patrols, each man taking his turn at patrolling all night around and around the ice floe, on his skis, looking for open water. The mental strain during this period was terrific, for we never knew when the cake we were on might break beneath us.

On June 2nd, at 5 P.M., we decided that our slip was worthy a trial. We started up the motors and taxied across the floe and down the slip, but we had built our slip too steep, and, therefore, not having enough speed, the plane simply sagged through the ice and for one thousand meters we merely plowed through it. We shut off the motors and prepared to spend the night in the lead.

At midnight I was awakened by Captain Amundsen

yelling that the plane was being crushed. I could plainly hear the pressure against the metal sides. We lost no time in getting everything out onto some solid ice near by, and by working the plane up and down permitted the incoming ice to close in beneath her from both sides. It was a narrow escape. We had expected the plane to be crushed like an egg-shell. Riiser-Larsen's only comment after the screwing stopped was, "Another chapter to be added to our book!" Before morning our first heavy fog set in. The Arctic summer was upon us. From then on the fog hung over us like a pall and for the remainder of our stay in the Arctic we were never free from it, although we were always able to see the rim of the sun through it and knew that above it the sky was clear and the sun shining brightly, but we could not rise into it. With the coming of the fogs the temperature rose to freezing.

We were gradually working our way over towards where the N. 24 was lying. During the day we would level off a new course, but there was not sufficient wind in which to rise, and as usual our heavily loaded plane broke through the thin ice,—

> "*Trailing like a wounded duck, working out her soul,*

.   .   .   .

Felt her lift *and felt her sag, betted when she'd break;*

. . . .

Wondered every time she raced if she'd stand the shock."

The N. 25 started leaking so badly from the pressure she received the other night that Captain Amundsen and I were obliged to pitch our tent on the floe upon which the N. 24 still lay with her nose on the ice floe, as we left her, but she had now listed sideways, so that the tip of one wing was firmly imbedded in the freshly frozen ice around her. During the past few days the ice had been freezing in from both sides, forming a long, narrow lane in front of N. 24, but parts of this lane had bent into a curve. It was a narrow, crooked passage, but Riiser-Larsen felt that it offered one more opportunity for a take-off. He taxied N. 25 forward, narrowly escaping an accident. As he slowed up to negotiate the curve, the nose broke through the ice with the reduced speed. The plane suddenly stopped and lifted its tail into the air. We jumped out and hacked away the ice until the plane settled on an even keel. We dared not remain where we were because the main body of the pack was fast closing in upon us from both sides.

At two o'clock the next morning we commenced

work on an extension of our previous course and continued on throughout the day and on into the following night. It was a tremendous task, as the ice was covered with tightly frozen lumps, old pressure-ridges of uplifted ice cakes. Hacking away with our short-handled pocket-ax and ice anchor was such back-breaking work that we were compelled to do it on our knees most of the time. The sweat was rolling down my face and blurred my snow-glasses, so that I was obliged to take them off for a couple of hours. I paid the penalty by becoming snow-blind in one eye. Dietrichson was not so fortunate. He was badly attacked in both eyes, and had to lie in the tent in his sleeping-bag for two days with his eyes bandaged and suffering acutely from the intense inflammation.

We awoke on the morning of June 5th, tired and stiff, to look upon the level track we had so frantically labored to prepare, but saw in its place a jumbled mass of upturned ice blocks. With the destruction of our fourth course our position was now desperate. But we would hang on till the vital decision would have to be made as to whether or not we should abandon N. 25 and make for the Greenland coast while there were yet sufficient provisions left. But we had come here on wings, and I know we all felt only wings could take us back to civilization. If we could only find a floe of sufficient area from which to take off, that was our difficulty.

In the early morning of June 6th Riiser-Larsen and Omdal started out into the heavy fog with the grim determination of men who find themselves in desperate straits, to search for what seemed to us all the unattainable. We saw no more of them till evening. Out of the fog they came, and we knew by their faces, before they uttered a word, that they had good news. Yes, they had found a floe! They had been searching through the fog, stumbling through the rough country. Suddenly the sun broke through and lit up one end of a floe, which became our salvation, as Riiser-Larsen put it. It was a half mile off, and it would be necessary to build a slip to get out of the lead and bridge two ice cakes before reaching the desired floe.

The main body of the pack was now only ten yards away. Immediately behind the N. 25 a huge ice wall was advancing slowly, inch by inch, and fifteen minutes after we started the motors the solid ice closed in over the spot where our plane had lain. We were saved.

We worked our way slowly up to where we meant to build the slip, using a saw to cut out the ice ahead where it was too heavy for the plane to break through. After six hours of steady toil we had constructed our

49

slip and had the plane safe up on floe No. 1. That
night of June 6th we slept well, after the extra cup
of chocolate that was allowed us to celebrate our narrow escape.

The next morning began the most stupendous task
we had yet undertaken; cutting a passage through a
huge pressure-ridge, — an ice wall fifteen feet thick
which separated floe No. 1 from floe No. 2, — and
then bridging between floe No. 1 and floe No. 2 two
chasms fifteen feet wide and ten feet deep, separating
the two floes from one another. In our weakened condition this was a hard task, but we finished it by the
end of the second day. Crossing the bridge between
the floes was exciting work. The sustaining capacity
of such ice blocks as we could manage to transport and
lay in the water could not be great. The heavier blocks
which we used for a foundation were floated into place
in the sea and left to freeze — as we hoped they would
— into a solid mass during the night. When the time
came, we must cross at full speed, if we were not to
sink into the sea, and then instantly stop on the other
side, because we had taken no time to level ahead, so
great was our fear that the ice floes might drift apart
during the operation of bridging. We made the pas-
sages safely and were at last upon the big floe. In
order to take advantage of the south wind, which had
continued to blow ever since the day of our landing,

we leveled a course across the shortest diameter of this cake, which offered only three hundred meters for a take-off. But before we completed our work the wind died down. Nevertheless we made a try, but merely bumped over it and stopped just short of the open lead ahead. Our prospects did not look good. The southerly winds had made the deep snow soft and soggy. But it was a relief to know that we were out of the leads, with our plane safe from the screwing of the pack-ice.

It was June 9th, and now began the long grind of constructing a course upon which our final hopes must rest. If we failed there was nothing left. My diary shows the following entry for June 10th:— "the days go by. For the first time I am beginning to wonder if we must make the great sarifice for our great adventure. The future looks so hopeless. Summer is on. The snows are getting too soft to travel over and the leads won't open in this continually shifting ice."

Riiser-Larsen looked the ground over and decided that we must remove the two and a half feet of snow right down to the solid ice and level a track twelve meters wide and four hundred meters long. It was a heartbreaking task to remove this wet summer snow with only our clumsy wooden shovels. It must be thrown clear an additional six meters to either side, so as not to interfere with the wing stretch. After but a few shovelfuls we stood weak and panting gazing disheartened at the labor ahead.

One problem was how to taxi our plane through the wet snow and get it headed in the right direction. We dug down to the blue ice, and now we were confronted with a new difficulty. The moist fog, which came over us immediately, melted the ice as soon as it was exposed. We found that by working our skis underneath the plane we were able finally to get it to turn, but after splitting a pair of skis we decided to take no more chances that way. In desperation we now tried stamping down the snow with our feet and found that it served the purpose admirably. By the end of our first day of shoveling down to the blue ice, we had succeeded in clearing a distance of only forty meters, while with the new method we were able to make one hundred meters per day. We adopted a regular system in stamping down this snow. Each man marked out a square of his own, and it was up to him to stamp down every inch in this area. We figured that at this rate we would have completed our course in five days.

During the first day's work we saw our first sign of animal life since the seal popped his head up out of the lead where we first landed. Somebody looked up from his work of shoveling snow to see a little auk flying through the fog overhead. It came out of the south and was headed northwest. Next day two weary geese flopped down beside the plane. They must have thought that dark object looming up through the fog in all the expanse of desolate white looked friendly. They seemed an easy mark for Dietrichson, but the rich prize was too much for his nerves and he missed. The two geese ran over the snow a long distance as if they were not anxious to take wing again. They too came from the south and disappeared into the northwest. We wondered if there could be land in that direction. It was an interesting speculation.

On the 14th our course was finished. Then Riiser-Larsen paced it again and was surprised to find that instead of four hundred meters it was five hundred. When he informed Amundsen of this fact, the Captain was quick to remark that one million dollars could not buy that extra hundred meters from him, and we all agreed that it was priceless.

On the evening of the 14th, after our chocolate, and with a southerly wind still blowing — this was a tail-wind on this course and of no help to us — we decided to make a try. But we only bumped along and the plane made no effort to rise. What we needed to get off with was a speed of one hundred kilometers per hour. During all our previous attempts to take off, forty kilometers had been the best we could do. On this trial we got to sixty, and Riiser-Larsen was hopeful. It was characteristic of the man to turn in his seat as we jumped out and remark to me: "I hope you are not disappointed, Ellsworth. We'll do better next time." That calm, dispassionate man was ever the embodiment of hope.

That night it was my watch all night. Around and around the ice-cake I shuffled, with my feet thrust loosely into the ski straps and a rifle slung over my shoulder, on the alert for open water. We were always afraid that the ice-cake might break beneath us. It was badly crevassed in places. Many times during that night, on my patrol, I watched Riiser-Larsen draw himself up out of the manhole in the top of the plane to see how the wind was blowing. During the night, the wind had shifted from the south and in the morning a light breeze was blowing from the north. This was the second time during our twenty-five days in the ice that the wind had blown from the north. We had landed with a north wind — but were we to get away with a north wind? That as the question. The temperature during the night was —1.5° c. and the snow surface was crisp and hard in the morning. We now were forced to dump everything that we could spare. We left one of our canvas canoes, rifles, cameras, field-glasses; we even discarded sealskin parkas and heavy ski-boots, replacing them with moccasins. All we dared retain was half of our provisions, one canvas canoe, a shotgun and one hundred rounds of ammunition.

Then we all climbed into the plane and Riiser-Larsen started up. Dietrichson was to navigate. The plane began to move! After bumping for four hundred meters the plane actually lifted in the last hundred meters. When I could feel the plane lifting beneath me I was happy, but we had had so many cruel disappointments during the past twenty-five days that our minds were in a state where we could feel neither great elation nor great suffering. Captain Amundsen had taken his seat beside Riiser-Larsen, and I got into the tail.

For two hours we had to fly through the thick fog, being unable either to get above or below it. During all this time we flew slowly, with a magnetic compass, a thing heretofore considered to be an impossibility in the Arctic. Dietrichson dropped down for drift observations as frequently as possible. The fogs hung so low that we were compelled to fly close to the ice, at one time skimming over it at a height of but one hundred feet. Finally we were able to rise above the fog and were again able to use our "Sun Compass."

Southward we flew! Homeward we flew! One hour — two hours — four, six hours. Then Feucht yelled back to me in the tail, "Land!" I replied, "Spitzbergen?" - "No Spitzbergen, no Spitzbergen!" yells back Feucht in his broken English. So I made up my mind that it must be Franz-Josefs-Land. Anyway, it was land, and that meant everything!

Our rationing regulations were now off, and we all started to munch chocolate and biscuits.

For an hour Riiser-Larsen had noticed that the stabilization rudders were becoming more and more difficult to operate. Finally they failed to work completely and we were forced down on the open sea, just after having safely passed the edge of the Polar pack. We landed in the sea, after flying just eight hours, with barely ninety liters of gasoline in our tanks, one half hour's fuel supply. The sea was rough, and we were forced to go below and cover up the man-holes, for the waves broke over the plane.

I had eaten seven cakes of chocolate when Feucht yelled, "Land ahead!" But I was now desperately ill and cared little what land it was so long as it was just land. After thirty-five minutes of taxi-ing through the rough sea, we reached the coast.

In we came — in the wash of the wind-whipped tide.

"*Overloaded, undermanned, meant to
founder, we
Euchred God Almighty's storm, bluffed the
Eternal Sea!*"

How good it felt to be on solid land again as we

threw ourselves down on a large rock, face upward to the sun, uncertain as to where we really were.

And what a change the interval of twenty-five days had wrought in its appearance. When we left, on May 21st, Spitzbergen was buried deep in snow, but now, on June 15th, the barren sun-warmed coast-line echoed to the shrill cries of little auks and gulls, while deep in the sheltering arms of the fjords, eider-duck and geese were mating and building their nests, all happily oblivious to the kingdom of silence and death that lay so close at hand, for plainly visible on the northern horizon lay the great fields of loose-moving ice over which we had flown for nearly an hour on our northward journey, before reaching the solid "pack."

The story of our six hundred mile flight from Spitzbergen out over the Polar Sea to 87°44′ North Latitude is now a matter of history, but history does not record the feelings of the six men who, after drifting about in the ice for twenty-five days, returned to solid land again; subdued, saddened, and perhaps humbled by the experience. We had been taught our inconsequence, our insignificance, in the presence of the great elements. But man is perhaps after all an emotional animal; and easily brought to his knees.

We got out our sextant and found that one of our position lines cut through the latitude of Spitzbergen.

While we were waiting to take our second observation for an intersection, three hours later, some one yelled, "A sail!"— and there, heading out to sea, was a little sealer. We shouted after them and put up our flag, but they did not see us, and so we jumped into our plane and with what fuel we had left taxied out to them. They were after a wounded walrus that they had shot seven times in the head, otherwise they would have been gone long before. They were over-joyed to see us. We tried to tow the plane, but there was too much headwind, so we beached her in Brandy Bay, North Cape, North-East-Land, Spitzbergen, one hundred miles east of our starting point at King's Bay.

We slept continuously during the three days in the sealer, only waking to devour the delicious seal meat steaks smothered in onions and the eider-duck egg omelets prepared for us.

The homage that was accorded us upon our return to civilization will ever remain the most cherished memory of our trip. We took steamer from King's Bay for Norway on June 25th, after putting our plane on board, and nine days later arrived at Horten, the Norwegian Naval Base, not far from Oslo.

On July 5th, with the stage all set, we flew N. 25 into Oslo. It was difficult to realize that we were in the same plane that had so recently been battling in the midst of the Arctic ice. Good old N. 25! We dropped down into the Fjord amid a pandemonium of frantically shrieking river craft and taxied on through the wildly waving and cheering throngs, past thirteen fully manned British battleships, and as I listened to the booming of the salute from the Fort and looked ahead at the great silent expectant mass of humanity that waited to greet us, I was overcome with emotion and the tears rolled down my face. At that moment I felt paid in full for all that I had gone through.

"Who can describe," says Amundsen, "the feelings which arose within us as we of the N. 25 flew in, over the flag-bedecked capital, where thousands upon thousands of people stood rejoicing? Who can describe the sights that met us as we descended to the water surrounded by thousands of boats? The reception on the quay? The triumphant procession through the streets? The reception at the Castle? And then, like a shining crown set upon the whole, Their Majesties' dinner at the Castle. All belongs to remembrance — the undying memory of the best in a lifetime."

Amundsen made his first public lecture on his polar flying expedition in the National Theatre at Oslo, August 14th. Among those present were the King, the Queen, Prince Olav, and the American Minister to Norway, Mr. Laurits Swenson. Amundsen paid a glowing tribute to his American companion, Ellsworth, "without whose generosity the expedition would never have taken place," and emphasized that when he saved Dietrichson and Omdal from drowning he saved the whole expedition, and he therefore deeply appreciated the King's act in conferring on Ellsworth the Gold Medal for the saving of life.

CHAPTER III.

"Aeluropus Melanoleucus"

By KERMIT ROOSEVELT

About sixty years ago a French Missionary, Père David, while travelling in the little independent buffer state of Muping, traded from the natives the incomplete skin of a curious bear-like animal which scientists christened *Aeluropus melanoleucus*. Its lay name is the giant panda. A parti-colored bear, about the size of a black bear, the animal is strikingly colored. Its head and forequarters are white. Its legs are black and a black band runs around behind its shoulders, while the rest of its body is white. The correct classification of the animal had long been a cause for controversy in scientific circles. From the available skins it was impossible to say whether it was a bear, a panda, or belonged in a class by itself.

My brother and I determined to make the securing of a giant panda the main objective of an expedition which we were planning along the Chinese-Tibetan borderland. It was impossible to secure in advance any information regarding the exact whereabouts of the giant panda, or any thing concerning its habits and the best method of securing one. All we could do was

DENSE BAMBOO JUNGLES ARE THE HOME OF THE GIANT PANDA

to rely upon such information and aid as we could pick up along the route.

As a result of our enquiries we determined that the animal has a fairly wide area of distribution, but is to be found only in pockets, and is never abundant even in such situations. He lives in bamboo jungles at altitudes varying between six and fourteen thousand feet. We came to the conclusion that it could be safely assumed that where there was no bamboo there were no giant panda, or beishung, as the natives called them. Local information required careful checking for even after a detailed description of the animal, and showing a plate depicting it, we could not rely upon a native's word as to its presence in a district. Sometimes this was due to very hazy notions of coloration, and to the assumption that the white crescent on the chest of the black bear (*Ursus torquatus*) entitled it to be called a panda. At other times misinformation was wilful, either from the common impulse to give pleasant and agreeable news, or because the native counted on earning some money as guide before his deception could be discovered.

We were unable to account satisfactorily for the scarcity of the animal. The problem of food should not prove difficult to a giant panda, for there was always plenty of bamboo. The natives rarely molest him. This is particularly true among the Lolos who regard him as a sort of semi-divinity. The other wild game found in the same locality would not appear to prove destructive to the giant panda, for it would seem very doubtful if, under any circumstances, either the black or brown bear or the snow leopard would attack a giant panda.

To the best of our belief, the panda does not hibernate. We met with fresh sign in regions where brown and black bears were hibernating, and the one we shot was found in a locality where the brown and black bears had not awakened from their winter's nap. As a result of careful study of the skeleton of this animal, scientists have agreed that it does not belong to any known species, but is *sui generis*.

The first locality in which we came across unmistakable sign of the panda's existence was in Muping, but in spite of as arduous hunting as either of us had ever done, we were unable to discover fresh trails or any sign of it. In all our marchings, we were continually enquiring for the beast, but it was not until we approached the Lolo country that we received any encouragement. We were warned by the Chinese authorities that it would be most unwise to enter Lololand, for they are an independent race and do not permit the Chinese to pass through their territory. We felt, however, that if we took things quietly, we could gain their confidence and assistance.

Tzetati was the last large town in which we could hope to secure any information, but we were able to learn there little or nothing that seemed useful, and set off for Tsalo, a small Chinese village on the very border of Lololand. Our first day's march took us to a little hamlet called Singchang. Here we were pleasantly surprised to find two French priests from the Catholic Mission at Fulin, Fathers Bocat and Flahntez. The former had spent eighteen years in China, the latter was but newly arrived. They were on a tour of inspection of their native Catholic congregations.

We had with us a flask of Benedictine which we had brought to drink with local headmen when opening relations. It was genuine pleasure to share some of it with these French priests, to whom it might recall pleasant evenings in their far-distant France, a land which neither would be likely to revisit, for these Fathers come out to dedicate their lives to their work, and renounce all thought of ever returning.

They both gave rather depressing accounts of the Lolo country, saying that it was greatly disturbed, and that they never travelled there and did not consider it safe. One of their Chinese priests had been captured not many months since on the borderland of the very country toward which we were headed, and his rescue had only been brought about after many difficulties and much negotiating. We assured them that we would take every precaution before entering the uncertain territory. Neither could give us any encouragement about the existence of the giant panda, and one of us sadly quoted,

> *"Till instead of the Kalends of Greece, men said,*
> *When Crook and his darlings come back with*
> *the head!"*

We had not been long on the road before one of our mules lost his footing and went spinning down the mountainside. Fortunately he brought up in a clump of thick bushes before any serious harm had been done, and half an hour later we had him back on the trail. By native wireless we learned that our main caravan, which we had left at Tzetati to pursue its way along the main travelled Chinese route, had met with a similar accident, but with a less fortunate outcome. The mule had rolled down into a stream. It was killed by the fall, but the load was salvaged. Throughout this trip we had found the "native wireless," very deficient, for we often learned nothing of people and events about which in Africa or Mesopotamia I would have been informed with speedy certitude by that unexplained method by which in the negro quarters in the South the results of the battles in the War of the Rebellion were known long before their masters in the Big House had heard.

"The wind from the brier-patch brought him news
That never went walking in white men's shoes
And the grapevine whispered its message faster
Than a horse could gallop across a grave,
Till, long ere the letter could tell the master,
The doomsday rabbits had told the slave."

We passed through several Lolo hamlets, and in one of them picked up a fine-looking Lolo, Mooka, as a guide. He belonged to the serf class and we had to obtain the consent of his master. Slavery is still in full force among the Lolos, but there is not the relationship between master and man that we commonly associate with the condition. Instead, there is a friendly companionship, and the sharing of food-bowl and wine-cup is often seen.

At one village in which we made enquiries we met with a rather cold reception. Our questions regarding game were parried with demands to be told what were in our loads and how many rifles we had with us.

The little Chinese outpost of Tsalo lies in a fertile valley among fields of corn and wheat and poppies. The headman was busy in his fields gathering poppy pods. He was evidently an opium addict. He knew little or nothing of the country ahead, although he said he understood that takin were to be found in the neighborhood of a Lolo village a day's march distant. Of the panda he could give us no word.

65

We were unfortunate in our choice of a lodging, for no sooner had we crawled into our bedding rolls than we heard the moaning of several sick people, and Hsuen came in to ask if we had any medicine for small-pox. He explained that there was an epidemic in the village and that in the next and only other room there was a poor woman who had lost one child and was now caring for her baby who was down with the disease. It is indeed distressing to hear the plaints of a sick child whom one is unable to help. There are times when any traveller, called upon for help in a hopeless case, may give a harmless pill in the hopes it may cause a fictitious relief or comfort, but with a dying infant such a procedure seems only heartless. A wretched woman in the next house and separated only by a thin partition was moaning and calling out in her delirium. The smell which drifted in from the courtyard beggared description. To add to Ted's discomforts he was suffering from the effects of bad food or water.

Altogether, when morning came we were more than ready for an early start. The Chinese headman had asked us to write him, taking all responsibility for our journey upon our own shoulders. We were afraid that to do so might cause him to pass on the word that we were any one's prey; we therefore refused, telling him that while we didn't require an escort, he might send one if he wished. Eleven militia turned up; two returned after accompanying us five or six miles, but the remainder proved a good lot, always ready to help or do any little odd job when called upon. We gave each man fifteen cents wine money a day. Just as we were leaving a man came along with a pony he wished to sell; an upstanding little bay, a four-year-old. We bought it for nine dollars.

Three hours out Hsuen, who was indefatigable in his wayside enquiries for news of game, came up in great excitement. Only last night, he said, a man had come to a house we had just passed asking the loan of a rifle to protect the beehives of his village from the raids of a beishung, or white bear, the native name for the panda. It appeared that a month ago this animal had paid a visit to the apiary, and he had wounded it. Now it had returned. Unable to borrow the rifle the villager had only just left to return to his house. Having been unable to secure even the vaguest news of the beast since leaving Muping, we had almost abandoned hope that there were any beishung in the country. This, therefore, certainly required looking into, and after verifying the report we made arrangements to follow up the trail.

We continued along for a couple of hours to a few houses known as Kooing Ma. We found that a name usually referred to a group of hamlets scattered about within a radius of several miles. Here we got in touch with the local headman and converted suspicion into friendship through the presentation of an axe and a Homburg hat, followed up by a leisurely gossip over a glass of Benedictine. It was decided that we should leave our mules here, for the trail to the panda village could be negotiated only by porters. Ten villagers were drafted in, to depart early in the morning.

We had gathered unto us at Tsalo a nondescript and rather shady appearing individual whom Hsuen named to us as a "brother-man." He was really a sub-species of the genus entrepreneur, so common throughout China. They live from the proceeds of acting as intermediary in dealings of every description. This particular "brother-man" was a Lolo who lived among the Chinese, and added to his liaison work, it was suspected, the distasteful post of spy. At Kooing Ma he was on his mettle to secure information of all sorts for us, and the first bit of news he produced was to the effect that the Lolos regarded the giant panda as a supernatural being, a sort of demi-god. This was discouraging, particularly since he added that he did not believe that they would take us hunting, for he was certain that the villagers themselves never attempted to kill a panda, except in defense of their beehives, and even in that case they tried only to wound the marauder and frighten it off.

68

"AELUROPUS MELANOLEUCUS"

This situation was not as disheartening as it might have been, for I had already had experience among natives, who, while owing to religious scruples unwilling themselves to kill a particular animal, were ready enough to aid a foreign hunter. We determined to approach the subject cautiously and carefully to avoid offending any native sensibilities.

We were quartered in a clean native hut, filled with enormous bowls of grain. The sides were made of split bamboo and the roof was tiled with pine slabs, which failed to make it completely waterproof to the heavy rain that fell during the night. At half-past three we were awakened by a rooster that thought he had discovered daylight and would not let the matter drop. He seemed to be sharing our hut, so Ted crawled out of his blankets and after a short search announced he had found a hen in a basket sitting on some eggs. I protested that a hen could not crow, but he disregarded my protest, and quoting the line about "crowing hens" to bear him out, he deposited the vainly complaining hen, basket and all, outside in the rain. All was quiet for a time, and then the crowing recommenced. Both of us hopped up, and our search was rewarded by discovering two roosters hidden away behind a mountainous pile of baskets. With my stick I rooted them out, while Ted directed them through the door, expediting their passage. Once more in our

69

blankets we prepared for the few remaining hours of sleep, when a mournful but none the less loud crowing announced that the disconsolate fowls had taken refuge under the eaves within a few feet of Ted's head. There was nothing further to be done.

In the morning we gathered eleven villagers to serve as porters. Unaccustomed to the work, they could carry only very light loads, and even so would go but a short distance before sitting down for a rest and a smoke. All the Lolos we met were inveterate smokers. They hollowed pipes out of stones; some were white, others green, and many were made from a red stone which closely resembled the red pipestone used by the American Indians. I bought specimens of the different sorts, and once was the innocent cause of what threatened to be a riot. A woman had brought me a rather well-made green pipe with a brass stem; I had agreed to purchase it, when a man pounced upon it, and started haranguing the woman. The excitement became general, each party gathering vociferous adherents. It was some time before things were sufficiently quieted down for me to learn that the man claimed that the pipe had been stolen from him. At length it was sifted down to the statement that he had lost the pipe a year ago on the trail, and the woman had found it. Finders were adjudged keepers, and the sale was concluded.

The distance from Kooing Ma to Kooing Hai is
short, as the crow flies, but the trail wound round
and about, and there were rivers to cross and steep
ravines to negotiate, so that it was not until two in the
afternoon that we came to the first of the group of
houses that go to make up Kooing Hai. We had taken
four soldiers, leaving the others with the mules. We
also had Mooka and the son of a neighboring head
man.

The mountainsides were glorious with rhododen-
drons, varying in hue from deep purple to white.
Pink was the prevailing color. In places the ground
was sprinkled with small blue flowers of the orchid
family. Blue lilies, forget-me-nots, primroses, and a
diminutive yellow blossom dotted the path side. We
were climbing up a valley, and as the altitude increased the crops were noticeably less advanced.

At moments it did not look as if we should meet
with a friendly reception. As we reached the hamlet
farthest up the valley, designated as our halting place,
the inhabitants took to the mountainside, and one
man was very visible, levelling a rifle at us. Our con-
ductors succeeded in smoothing things out, but only
with a good deal of difficulty, and it was not a friendly
appearing delegation that dropped down to talk things
over with us. I think it was the Chinese soldiers that
were largely responsible for the distrust. Hsuen told

us that among the Lolos we were usually taken for what he translated as "holy fathers," as they call Catholic priests. This honor was due to our beards.

Throughout the expedition we found that it was impossible to tell what sort of gift would prove a success. The knives and axes which had been a flat failure in Muping were now of the greatest service, and went a long way to clear the horizon. On the other hand, the cheap field-glasses from which we had expected much were firmly rejected. The offer of a glass of Benedictine stood us in good stead. The head-man of the village was won over, but his tall, handsome old father did not appear to yield quite so readily to our attempted blandishments. It was evident that except in defense of their property they did not care to attack the giant panda. We verified yesterday's story of the raid on the apiary, which stood close to the headman's hut and was protected by a strong fence. It had taken place a month previous. We were also told that six years ago a beishung had been killed during a honey raid. This was the only record they could give us of one being killed.

All the afternoon and throughout the night it rained. In the morning the skies were overcast, but no rain was falling. Ten Lolo hunters with an equal number of dogs gathered outside our tent, which we had pitched close to a hut. We set out at half-past six

for the mountains. A couple of hours' climbing took
us up among the bamboos, and we were soon drenched
to the skin and shivering with the cold. Remnants of
the winter snows lay in patches. The Lolos, shrouded
in the brown or black capes they weave from sheep's
wool, seemed happy enough. They appeared to feel
that there was a very good chance of bagging a panda,
although we could not share in their optimism. As
we made our way through the dense jungle along a
ridge, we twice heard the dogs running something
below us. In neither case did it come to anything. A
halt was called and a fire was lit with much difficulty.
One of the Lolos took a handful of moss into the
centre of which he placed a bit of smouldering tinder.
By dint of incessant blowing, undertaken in relays, a
flame was eventually produced.

Several of the Lolos had kept to the valley on
either side of our ridge, and we had not been warming
ourselves for long before a series of unintelligible
shouts informed our companions that the dogs were
running a sounder of swine. We did not want to shoot
pig, but after a hurried debate we decided that it
would be better for our future chances, in keeping our
hunters keyed up, if we shot game for them when an
opportunity arose that did not conflict with our beishung hunting. Such was very obviously the present
situation, for with their dogs off after wild pig our

Lolos could no longer hunt anything. The scramble down into the valley was most precipitous; it was bad enough in the forested spots, but when we came to bare spaces it became all but impossible. Our hopes of finding the going better along the bed of the torrent were quickly dashed. The stream thought nothing of a forty-foot drop, but to clamber down the slippery perpendicular rock slides, securing a precarious toe hold in a fissure or grasping the doubtful root of some plant, proved very difficult for us. The results of several falls entailed nothing more serious than abrasions and bruises and sprains, and we thought ourselves lucky on emerging on a native trail where the ravine débouched out into the main valley. Rain and sleet were now falling, and most of the dogs had abandoned the pursuit of the pigs. After some further futile climbing our hunters decided to call it a day, and we returned to our tent with a practical working knowledge of the country and its difficulties.

By this time the headman had become definitely friendly, and we sat about the fire discussing ways and means of securing game, drifting now and then into more general topics. Hsuen's choice of words and *tournures de phrase* were a constant delight and capable of cheering the most gloomy moments. The subject had as usual turned to sickness and to the medicine of which it required a constant well-balanced and calculating effort to preserve any of our small stock. Hsuen translated, "Headman say he got ghost in head. Ghost make itch all time. Other people's head not itch, so headman know he got ghost." Ted, with great ceremony, presented a small box of cold cream, saying that if well rubbed in, it would lay the ghost. We were next told of a ghost that every January caused great mortality among the children. This was undoubtedly pneumonia, and a more difficult apparition to deal with.

The rain fell continuously all night, and several holes in the tent made it an uncomfortable residence but there was no room in any nearby hut, so we had to make the best of it. Dawn broke cold and gray, with no pause in the rain. We thought it extremely unlikely that any Lolo would stir from his hut, but we were soon undeceived, for during the next hour no less than thirty-two men straggled in, each leading a dog on a string. The dogs were identical with those that we used in the Muping country. A good deal of rain had found its way into the tent during the night so that we were a bedraggled lot, even before starting; not that it made any difference, for half an hour would have sufficed thoroughly to saturate us with mud and water.

Before setting off for the mountains our hunters

"made medicine." The Lolos carve no likenesses of their gods. To cure a sick man they hold services and beat drums, or burn holes in the scapular bone of a sheep, but nowhere did we see idols of any description. Two of our hunters took sticks and whittled notches, muttering the while. As far as we could gather the main purpose was the determining of a propitious locality for the hunt. Hsuen looked sagely on. Turning to us he remarked, "They pray God," then shrugging his shoulders, "Perhaps it do good, I not know."

Aside from the fact that we burrowed our way through a different bamboo jungle along a different ridge, there was little to differentiate this day's hunting from the previous. The dogs separated and presumably hunted the valleys on either side. On each day we came across beishung sign, but in neither case did we feel that there was more than one animal indicated. From our observations we were certain that there were very few panda about, far less than in Muping. At noon we built a fire and from the folds of their cloaks the Lolos drew forth round lumps of bread liberally studded with beans. Among the hunters one old fellow particularly interested us. He must have been in the late sixties, and was looked upon by the others as a mine of hunting lore. His counsel weighed heavily in the decisions regarding the disposition of our forces. Somewhere enroute he had gathered some white fungus which he roasted in the embers, ate, and appeared greatly to enjoy.

Once or twice the dogs picked up the trail of some animal, but they never held it for long. Aside from beishung signs of questionable age, all we saw were some musk-deer tracks, and a number of places where wild hogs had been rooting.

The result of the evening conference was a determination to put in a final hunt on the following morning, and if nothing came of it, to move further on to where we had been told takin were to be found. We paid our Lolo hunters from fifteen to thirty cents a day, offering a large reward to the man who could first point out a panda, and lesser rewards to any others who should really have had a part in the successful hunt.

The villagers enriched themselves through us in other ways. We bought a sheep and eggs and some wine bowls and many stone pipes. One of the hunters had a curious bamboo musical instrument which he played by holding it against his teeth and blowing upon it, while he snapped the taut bamboo slivers with his fingers. We asked Hsuen to get us a couple, and he wagged his head and said, with a twinkle in his eye:

"That very bad thing, I tell you story some day all

about it. It kill many people, oh, seven hundred." Pressed to continue, he explained: "This country, same as everywhere, Father Mother he say I got son, I find him wife. He find wife. Girl's mother, he find wife. Perhaps son see other girl he like. He play music her like this. She play music him. He say 'My Father Mother say marry girl I no like.' She say, 'My Father Mother say I marry man I no like.' He say, 'I like you. You like me?' She say, 'I like you.' He say, 'We go top big mountain.' They go top big mountain, they play music, they tie together big knot round both necks, they both hang to tree. Oh, many people, seven hundred, die. That very bad."

Our next morning's hunt was a repetition of those of the two previous days. Again we climbed a ridge. This time instead of rain and sleet we had snow, but the effect was much the same. We found no beishung sign. Ted saw a pheasant, and I caught a fleeting glimpse of a large squirrel.

We had sent Hsuen ahead with our kit to Kooing Ma, telling him to gather the mules and go on to Litzaping, a village near which we had been told that takin were to be found. We followed at the termination of our hunt, and reached Litzaping just before dark.

Four headmen gathered to greet us. We first gave each a liqueur glass of Benedictine. We then bought

some native wine which we poured into bowls that
circulated among the headmen and their dependents.
They were a fine, stalwart lot, and very friendly. We
had heard that the Lolos were heavy drinkers, but
we saw no indications of their being so. Their wine is
usually made from corn. It varied greatly in quality,
though none of it could really be called an agreeable
beverage.

Our friends were unanimous in saying that there
were very few takin about. We had heard there were
many near a mountain named Tsumei Kwa. This they
denied; one and all advising us to go on to Yehli,
where they said there were many takin and an occasional giant panda. It was decided that we should send
back the Chinese soldiers and take with us a son of
each of the headmen. The Lolos said that with the
soldiers accompanying us we might find ourselves in
difficulties, but that without them we would be safe.
Hsuen was by now thoroughly sick of the "brother-
man" to whom he referred sarcastically as "our dear
brother," but he was afraid he might do us harm if
sent back, and for several more days we gave way to
Hsuen's judgment. All of us were heartily glad
when, eventually, we arbitrarily forced him to turn
back.

On the 12th of April we set out for Yehli. A persistent rain was falling, which added to the difficulties

of the trail. Our pack animals consisted of our mules and two ponies. One of the latter missed his footing and started down the mountainside. A muleteer pluckily grabbed his head stall and went rolling over and over among the boulders until long after it had seemed impossible for him to hold on further. A most convenient dense clump of sturdy bushes prevented pony and packer from taking the final sheer plunge into the river that would have definitely ended the careers of both. We were delayed half an hour in lugging the pony back to the trail.

Twice during the march a halt was called while the muleteers turned into road-builders to overcome the work of a landslide. At length the valley opened up, and we had easy going. The country became more and more lovely; giant pine trees grew beside the path, and we finally rode out onto a great mountain meadow, with a wide grassy valley, hemmed in by well-forested mountains terminating in barren snowclad peaks. We felt that we might almost be back in the paradise of Tian Shan.

The hamlet at which we halted formed a part of the Yehli group. The cabins were large, and the ground about them was trampled with the feet of cattle and sheep. A heavy rain was falling and a dense fog soon shrouded the valley, making most welcome the pine-wood fire in the centre of the cabin.

"AELUROPUS MELANOLEUCUS"

We started immediately on our hunting "bundo-
bust." Two self-styled experts were summoned. One
was obviously a hunter, the other gave rise to doubts.
The former had shot takin, and produced a head in
proof. Both said that it was not too difficult to obtain
them, and both agreed that there were a few beishung
about, but that it would be almost impossible to get a
shot at one. So far so good. Next a unanimous opinion
was volunteered to the effect that it was impossible to
hunt in this weather. When asked when an improvement might be looked for, both announced that the
rain and sleet were in order at this time of year, and
it was not possible to foretell a clearing up. This was
indeed desolating, but Hsuen threw himself into the
breach, bringing every argument to bear. The difficulty was increased by the absence of the headman of
the valley. He had gone away on a journey, and the
date of his return was uncertain. At length Hsuen
made it clear that we could not await a change in
weather, and all chance of a golden egg would vanish
unless we were taken hunting on the morrow. Re-
luctantly the Lolos yielded. A new difficulty was encountered when we tried to secure four hunters so
that we could separate. The hunter with the aura of
doubt said that he would substitute his son for himself. He told us the boy was eighteen, but when we
had him paraded he was obviously no more than

twelve. After skilful sifting it developed that his sole qualification as a takin hunter lay in his having once eaten takin meat.

A shepherd brought in a very small wild pig, which he had found while tending his flocks in the hills. It was striped and spotted with white, and could not have been more than a few weeks old. It was dead, and conjured up visions of roast suckling pig at Thanksgiving dinners at Sagamore. We bought it for fifteen cents, and Hsuen's culinary efforts resulted in an undeniable success.

It was late before we had at long last straightened things out, and felt reasonably certain that four Lolos would be on hand in the morning. We then crawled up into a hay loft where we slept with the four heirs apparent of Litzaping who had come along with us as bodyguard.

Saturday, the 13th of April, dawned cold and overcast. It had snowed during the night and the floor of the valley was covered and the pine trees on the mountainsides were in conventional Christmas garb. We set off with four hunters, the takin-eating boy, and five slim black dogs. A thin misty rain set in. It was a cheerless beginning for what was destined to become our red-letter day. Four porters were to follow with our bedding rolls and those of the shikaries, for the programme called for a night or two *à la belle étoile* on the mountain where takin were reported.

Three or four miles took us past the clump of cabins belonging to A'Souza, the absent headman. At an equal distance further up the valley we turned off into a ravine. It was only a short way further on that we came upon giant panda tracks in the snow. The animal had evidently passed a goodish while before the snow ceased falling, but some sign that one of the Lolos found proved to be recent enough to thoroughly arouse all four natives. We had taken our ponies to ride until we should enter the jungle or the going become too difficult, and Mooka had come along to lead them back. It was now that he arose to the occasion and reached the high watermark of his value. The Lolos hesitated to follow the beishung both for religious scruples and because of the very definite instructions that we wished takin. We could gather that a conference was under way, but believed that it concerned ways and means only, and there is no telling what might have resulted had not Mooka, as we afterward learned, stepped into the breach and explained that above all else we wanted beishung.

This brought the conference to a close and we started off on the trail of the panda. It was not long before the dogs definitely demonstrated their utter futility. We passed some rat burrows in a small hollow. Four of our dogs lost all interest in anything

83

beyond and devoted their entire attention to the pursuit of the rats. The one that still remained with us trotted along at our heels baying until Ted caught it a shrewd clip with his stick. It retreated yowling into the forest and that was the last we saw of it.

We now settled down to the steady business of tracking. Only three of the Lolos continued with us. The beishung appeared to be travelling along in leisurely fashion, browsing on the bamboos as he went. The amount of sign that he left made us realize that we had been correct in making a conservative estimate of the number of beishung inhabiting the country beyond Muping, in which we hunted. Soon we came upon a boar's tracks superimposed on those of the giant panda. This continued for a mile or more. Our quarry had evidently been in no hurry. For a while he followed up the rocky bed of a torrent, then he climbed a steep slope, through a jig-saw puzzle of windfalls. The fallen logs were slippery with snow and ice. Here we could crawl through and under; there we had to climb laboriously around and over. The bamboo jungle proved a particularly unpleasant form of obstacle course, where many of the feathery tops were weighed down by snow and frozen fast in the ground. Drenched by rain and soaked by snow, whenever a moment's halt was called we alternately shivered and panted. For a few minutes the sun came out, and we were in dread that it would melt the tracks, but after a brief interval the murky clouds hid it again.

We had been following the trail for two and a half hours when we came to a more open jungle. Tall spruce trees towered their giant bulk above the bamboos. Lichen-covered alders were dotted about. An occasional blue or yellow flower poked its head up where the snow lay lighter. Here the panda had turned his attention more seriously to provender. Under one tree he had made himself a nest of bamboos. His claw marks scored the bark, and we looked eagerly among the sturdy branches to see whether we could distinguish a black and white form crouching on a limb. His tracks led in many directions. The tough fibrous bamboos seemed to offer but an uninviting dehydrated repast at best, and to judge from the droppings they were difficult to digest. Below us in the valley we heard the dogs yawping on the trail of some animal, probably a hog. We earnestly wished them elsewhere, for we felt sure that the beishung had not gone much further before seeking some accustomed haunt to spend the sleepy daylight hours.

It was difficult to straighten out the trail. We cast first in one direction, then in another. Unexpectedly close I heard a clicking chirp. It might have been a bamboo snapping or the creaking of the interlocking branches of two trees swayed by the wind. I remembered the eager interest of the Muping hunters at hearing just such a sound. In that case the noise had really been made by trees. One of the Lolo hunters was now close to Mokhta Lone and me. Noiselessly he darted forward. He had not got forty yards before he turned back to eagerly motion to us to hurry.

As I gained his side he pointed to a giant spruce thirty yards away. The bole was hollowed, and from it emerged the head and forequarters of a beishung. He looked sleepily from side to side as he sauntered forth. He seemed very large, and like the animal of a dream, for we had given up whatever small hopes we had ever had of seeing one. And now he appeared much larger than life with his white head with black spectacles, his black collar and white saddle.

Ted had started in a different direction with another Lolo, so Mokhta Lone and I eagerly signalled him. Though in reality only a short time, it was a nerve-wracking wait. The giant panda, dazed by sleep, was not really aroused, and was walking slowly away into the bamboos. If frightened it could vanish like smoke in the jungle. As soon as Ted came up we fired simultaneously at the outline of the disappearing panda. Both shots took effect. Not knowing where his enemies were, he turned toward us, floundering through the drifted snow that lay in a hollow on our left. He was but five or six feet from Mokhta Lone when we again fired. He fell, but recovered himself and made off through the densely growing bamboos. We knew he was ours, so although the Lolos had all along told us that a beishung was not an animal to be feared, we used caution in following the trail. A couple of the dogs that had been hunting in the valley below now came bounding by us, but they very evidently did not share their masters' opinions as to the innocuous character of the beishung. They trailed, howling, behind us and nothing could induce them to go ahead. No help, however, was needed, for the pursuit ended in seventy-five yards, when we found the animal dead. He was a splendid old male, the first that the Lolos had any record of as being killed in this Yehli region.

The shikaries, the Lolos, and ourselves held a mutual rejoicing, each in his own tongue. Our great good fortune could be credited only with much effort. We had hunted hard and long, usually in the face of every adverse circumstance. The previous evening conditions had seemed at their blackest, and it did not look as if we would be able to stir the Lolos from their homes. Now all was changed, and after so long holding aloof, the hunting gods had turned about and fashioned the unusual chain of circumstances that alone could enable us to shoot a giant panda, trailing him without dogs and with the crowning bit of luck that permitted us to fire jointly.

When the enthusiasm had subsided sufficiently to allow us to think of anything beyond the immediate results of the chase, there were other plans to be worked out. In the face of the rain and sleet, and handicapped by a badly burst case, I had packed my camera in my bedding. My first thought was to get it, so Ted stayed behind to struggle with transportation difficulties while I hurried down to the valley. As we slithered and slipped and barked our shins and knees, we kept up a running recapitulation of the details of the chase. When Mokhta Lone paused for breath I broke in and took up the tale. I later learned that Ted and Gaffer Sheikh had been similarly employed. Mokhta Lone insisted that the panda was a sahib, for unlike the bear it did not cry out when shot.

At length we reached A'Souza's lodge, where we hoped to find Hsuen and the mules. There was no sign of them. It was a blow, for it further dimmed any chance of successful photography. While trying to learn of Hsuen's whereabouts we sat for a few brief minutes at the hospitable hearth of Vooka, A'Souza's wife, who acted in his stead during his absence. She was a tall handsome woman, wearing the conventional hooded head-dress of Lolo women. She was smoking a long-stemmed pipe with a heavy

stone bowl, that she later told us had belonged to her
mother and grandmother before her. Filling it with
tobacco she thrust it into the fire to top the bowl with
a pyramid of embers. Then she handed it ceremonially
to me, reminding me of a Red Indian passing the
peace pipe. One of her daughters brought half a
dozen eggs in a bowl made of takin hide.

There was, unfortunately, no time to be lost, so we
hurried back to our last night's halting-place. There
we found Hsuen, and hastily started the mules forward to A'Souza's. It was not until half past four that
I again found Ted and the beishung. My pursuit of
the camera had taken me on a fourteen-mile jaunt.
It was raining and sleeting, and numbed fingers made
but clumsy work with the camera. These Lolos were
unaccustomed to carrying loads, and Ted had had a
weary and discouraging time of it. For a while he
tried to float the panda down the stream; but after
struggling in the ice-bound water for a short time he
abandoned the attempt and gralloched the animal.
He had hoped to avoid doing so until after the camera
should have arrived. He found no sign that the panda
had varied its bamboo diet.

Great were the celebrations held that night at
A'Souza's. Vooka ordered a sheep to be slaughtered,
and resolutely refused to allow us to foot the bill.
Intermingled with it all, there was strongly pervading

an element of superstition. The beishung was at first
not permitted in the compound, and we were afraid
that we would have to skin it in the rain and snow and
mud. Religious scruples were at length so far relaxed
as to permit the shikaries to carry it into an isolated
hayloft. A deeply interested group surrounded us at
our work, but not an omnivorous Lolo of the lot
would touch a morsel of the flesh. Hsuen told us that
after we left a priest was to be sent for and an all-
embracing ceremony of purification would be held,
to cleanse the house and its surroundings from any
shadow that the death of the giant panda might cast
upon it.

The feasting lasted late. The sheep was quartered
and plunged into a huge cauldron that was raised on
three tall stones above the fire. A little later the par-
boiled meat was fished out and hacked into smaller
pieces. These were thrust back into the boiling water.
A silent ring of expectant Lolos lined the walls of the
big raftered building. They were shrouded in their
long capes, and it was as well, for there were many
chinks in the roughly shingled roof, and the rain fell
ever faster. When the sheep was ready, Vooka's servants ladled great chunks into wooden bowls, and
adding rice from a smaller cauldron, handed them
around among the guests. Soon wine was poured into a
wooden beaker and circulated through the throng. It

was in the main a silent gathering, lit by the flickering
fagots of pine that were thrust from time to time upon
the fire. With Vooka seated beside the fire, smoking
her long pipe and directing her retainers, the whole
might well have fitted a feudal feast in Europe in the
Middle Ages. Ted and I mixed a hot toddy from
the last of our flask of brandy and drank the health
of every one, starting with General Pereira, whose
attempts to shoot panda, made in the face of so many
difficulties, fortune had not favored.

It was late when we crawled up into the hayloft
where our bedding was laid out. Never were the
sleeping bags more gratefully welcome.

CHAPTER IV.

Taps for the Great Selous

By FREDERICK R. BURNHAM

In the crash of nations and the death of millions of brave men, it is difficult to accentuate the life or death of any single one, yet the character, life, and dramatic end of Frederick Courtney Selous warrants a special moment of thought by each of us who knew him in life. His career as a naturalist, author, pioneer, great hunter, soldier, and scout is so varied and colorful that I shall confine these pages to a few personal recollections among the many vivid ones formed in the early days when South Africa was sweating blood and struggling for her place in the sun.

When Rhodes, the towering genius of Africa, was suddenly confronted by a war with Lobengula, the most powerful black king in Africa, there was just a chance that a successful diversion could be made against Lobengula via Mafeking and the Mangwi Pass of the Matoppo Mountains. If this force could be made strong enough and move fast enough they *might* (accent on the might) be in time to divide the forces of the King and save the whole colony of Mashonaland from annihilation. The colonists were isolated by five hundred miles of bush veldt but were pitting their all in one little poorly equipped army of six hundred settlers carrying their entire equipment in twenty-two wagons. They had no base of supplies or place of retreat if defeated. They, like Pizarro and Cortez, when in doubt, attacked. These colonists did not believe in Chinese walls of defense but, when war was forced upon them, struck boldly for the King's capital with every fighting man able to put one foot ahead of the other. Latent strength of nations, like natural resources, does little good in a sudden emergency, and Africa's history is largely made up of sudden emergencies. Rhodes found the only force actually available was the B.B.P. (Bechuanaland Border Police) of 225 men. This was never a regular force but corresponded to the North West Mounted of Canada and at best was only a small force.

Rhodes taking 220 C.M.R. (Cape Mounted Rifle) and 225 B.B.P. secured the services of an Imperial officer of experience, Colonel Goold Adams. He also obtained the rather lukewarm support of King Khama, a supposedly friendly Christian king whose territory lay between the kingdom of the Matabele ruled by Lobengula and the Kalahari Desert. It is necessary to keep this in mind because Rhodes' little force could only attack King Lobengula by crossing King Khama's country. Even with this neutral terri-

tory open there were still left the long defiles of the
Matoppo Mountains before reaching the plateau on
which Bulawayo, the capital, was located.

Out of all the great Kaffir fighters, voertrekers and
scouts of South Africa that Rhodes could select he
chose Selous and I believe for judgment, skill, speed
and daring, this little known campaign of Selous, in
which the levies of King Khama deserted under fire,
is a good example of the kind of service so often per-
formed by him from early youth 'til his death on the
front when old and gray, two thousand miles north
and beyond the borderland as he knew it in his youth.

In this march into the defiles of the Matoppos to
aid the Mashonaland settlers, Selous himself was
wounded but did not give up command of his troop.

In this instance was witnessed the happy spectacle
of an Imperial officer who conceded that a colonial
knew something of his own people and a colonial
officer who realized that the Imperial traditions and
discipline of a thousand years were a wonderful asset
to take into any war, even against cunning savages.
So these two men, Goold Adams and Selous, a wonderful team — added the Boer, Captain Raaf, the
hero of many Kaffir wars, who, in command of 220
Cape Mounted Rifles, rushed north. This combined
force began their march October 11th, 1893. They
fought a clever series of battles and elusive actions

in the passes of the mountains. They conserved their own forces, yet drew off many thousands of King Lobengula's warriors from the settlers who, desperately advancing from Mashonaland under Dr. Jameson, fought their way to the plateau and captured the capital, Bulawayo.

Upon the fall of Bulawayo, it was my fortune to act as Scout for the Mashonaland forces. Captain White ordered me to report to Dr. Jameson. The following information was given me: "Rumors are that Goold Adams led by Selous is fighting hopelessly somewhere in the Mangwi Pass. He may be defeated and if so will fall back into Khamaland. Go and find him wherever he is and tell him we have taken Bulawayo, but not captured the King, that we must have every horse and man possible at once and, no matter what defeats he has had, to about face and attack. I will advance to Fig Tree, the head of the Mangwi Pass, if need be — to aid. After finding Goold Adams, take this letter to Rhodes and deliver it to C.O. at Tati."

It was all new country to me. Jameson gave me the pick of any horses or man in the force. I chose Ingram, the scout, and two courageous horses — for horses like men vary in this quality. These horses were handicapped by being barefooted. We now chose one mounted native interpreter whom we had tried out in several very tight corners before. The country swarmed with hostiles. We evaded them and all went well until the rain came, softening the already tender feet of our mounts. Then even our lion-hearted horses gave way, crippling along at a walk, but I cut from a native bull hide shield, found in an abandoned kraal, pieces of hide, and laced them on our horses' feet, an old American trapper's trick taught me in my boyhood and thus shod we found a loophole in the enemy's lines before Goold Adams and Selous and rode into headquarters in the Mangwi Pass. Selous was seriously wounded in the ribs but did not give up command nor did it dull his curiosity to minutely examine my method of shoeing horses, new to both himself and Goold Adams. As I dashed on down country to Tati, Selous and Adams advanced at once to Bulawayo, scattering the enemy and saving every horse possible.

The B.B.P. had been properly trained to take especial care of their horses and it was mostly from Goold Adams' little column that enough horses were chosen to make the final dash after King Lobengula into the jungles of the Shangani. Some wars are a struggle for fuel, some for rice, some for bread. This little war was for horse feed. Mounted we lived, dismounted we died. Selous knew where and how the Kaffirs buried grain around their old kraals and Goold Adams taught the troopers how to cut and carry even a wisp of grass or a handful of leaves for their mounts.

There was much rejoicing in Bulawayo when Selous led the little column into the great kraal of the King and Dr. Jameson gave him the medical care and rest needed to prepare him for his most important job which was soon to be.

Jameson had now gained his first objective, the capture of Bulawayo, but in a miniature way it might easily have been Moscow with "King Dikhop" to fight, instead of "King Frost." "King Dikhop" does not freeze your men but he slays your horses with a deadly sickness. The enemy had burned their capital with all its stores of ivory and provisions. King Lobengula was now in retreat into the jungles of the Shangani. The rains were upon us and soon would come the insidious attack upon our already worn out horses, today keen and excited at the crack of a gun, tomorrow listless, swollen headed and dead — Dikhop.

Jameson realized that for his little army to be dismounted in the heart of the enemy's country, with the King still at large and in command of thousands, meant that every settler in Mashonaland as well as his entire command would be annihilated. He, therefore, called for volunteers and selected 160 of the toughest horses and strongest men to follow the King. This force was commanded by Forbes and the heroic

Wilson who, with all his men, was so great in death and defeat that it resulted in the final surrender of the Matabele. The balance of the command under Forbes struggled for days up the Shangani, eating their dying horses and carrying their wounded. Two scouts, Ingram and Lynch, managed to get to Bulawayo with the news of the plight of Forbes' column. They were too weak and exhausted to be used as guides to find Forbes somewhere on the Shangani so Jameson took the wounded Selous to lead the rescue column. Rhodes and Jameson took as many men as could be spared from the captured Bulawayo and headed for the Shangani.

It was my particular work as scout to lead Forbes' column toward Bulawayo for we were fighting and retreating over country entirely unknown to every one in command. We had reached a point on the Shangani River that, by turning south-west, we should, if my calculations were correct, hit Inyati and again be in known country and only forty miles from Bulawayo and help.

On the afternoon of the 14th of December Capt. Raaf, the famous Boer, rode up beside me. He was the exhausted shadow of his former self and, although he must have known that his end was at hand, his one anxiety was to check up with me my reasons for leaving the Shangani at that point because he said every

yard of error in distance counted with our falling
men. As we were talking, my eye caught just a flicker
in the scrub and I soon saw the leaves shake again and
then in a moment over a little ridge rode the alert
Selous with our beloved Dr. Jim beside him and just
behind came Rhodes and a group of shouting fighting
men to our rescue — men who were then young
troopers and volunteers but most of them destined to
sway in years to come the fortunes of Rhodesia and
all South Africa. Selous had taken word for word
from Ingram the directions to cut our spoor and
did so without the loss of a mile of distance or an
hour's time, two elements that have to be considered
always in war with savages just as it is considered in
the Kriegspiel war game or in action on the Western
Front.

The rescue of our column was followed soon by the
death of the King in the jungles, the surrender of the
natives and the opening of the whole country to settlement and peace. This was the golden age of Rhodesia. Rhodes and Jameson were still alive and the
whole country prospered. Selous was given a big farm
of many thousand acres and settled down, as we all
thought, for a long, peaceful life after a very stirring
one of many years on the veldt. In reality the most
important pages of his life had not been turned.

Three years later, in 1896, came for Rhodesia those

terrible years that nearly every colony goes through. Out of her Pandora's box leaped Rinderpest which killed all cud chewing animals, locusts that ate up every living green thing, then a terrible uprising among the savage Matabele and, to cap it all, trouble with the Boers. It found our trusted leader, Rhodes, out of the country, while Jameson and all his men were either dead on the veldt or prisoners of war. Often these first colonies, like Rhodesia or our own Jamestown, are "sunk without a trace" from the pages of history. Sometimes they are preserved as by a miracle from extinction. In this instance, because of a handful of remarkable men who had caught the fire from Rhodes' torch, they carried on as if he had been personally leading them.

Well to the forefront in all this second war rode Selous and his troop day and night, sleepless and aggressive, heartening this one, helping that one, rescuing this group, reinforcing that one. The soft spoken, easy going Selous now moved like a lion of the old days when he was truly king.

After the war it was my good fortune to meet Theodore Roosevelt who was then Commissioner of Police of New York City. Almost the first question he shot at me was "Do you know Selous? I am greatly attracted to that man from what I have heard of him and what I have seen of his writings." I told Roosevelt that Selous was a writer who would not disappoint him, should they meet, and furthermore, he could take Selous on a camping trip, which is the acid test, and Selous would return from it in even higher esteem; that Selous represented what in those days was rather rare among our countrymen, a great hunter but not a killer, and that already he had joined his voice and pen to that small band of naturalists and sportsmen who were laying plans for the conservation of the wild life of Africa. Roosevelt said "We must invite him to visit the United States and make him a member of the Boone and Crockett Club." This wish was fulfilled as Selous later became a friend of Roosevelt and of every member of the Club.

Now I shall skip all those interesting years so well known to all our fellow members and partially made of record by Selous's accurate pen so devoid of the superlative, yet full of incidents that truly happened and a portrayal of things as they were.

We met once more in times of peace near the head of the Nile, each of us on an expedition having to do with the driving of a small stake in a deep jungle. We were both turning gray. Neither of us knew of the presence of the other in the country. It seemed as though our chances of meeting there and then were about equal to firing a shotgun out of a window at night into the sky and bringing down a silent winged owl. Yet unknown to either of us, Selous was then marking out the trails over which England, in her hour of need, would again call him to act as guide against a foe, this time a mighty one on the east coast of Africa. Germany had founded a strong colony and thoroughly drilled and disciplined a large native army. It was officered by experienced soldiers. They put up a wonderful defense and were not defeated until Jan Smuts, the Boer, one of the outstanding men of the Great War, came from South Africa with 50,000 men who threw in their lot with England and the Allies. This decided the issue for the great Colony of German East Africa but not until after many years of fighting and until, among their dead, the Allies marked the death of the man who pioneered an empire and who will be long remembered as one of the great path finders of the age, Frederick Courtney Selous. His last wish was fulfilled: "Death in action."

GIANT SABLE ANTELOPE

Group in the Academy of Natural Sciences of Philadelphia.

CHAPTER V.

Along the Livingstone Trail

By PRENTISS N. GRAY

The name of H. F. Varian is honored by every African hunter, not for his outstanding work as construction engineer of the Benguela Railway which connects the Katanga copper mines with the west coast, but for his discovery of the Giant Sable antelope within a small territory between the Luanda and Quanza Rivers in Portuguese West Africa. The Giant Sable of Angola differs principally from the common sable in its more massive horns that sweep in an imperious curve from head to flank. No other heads in all Africa can compare with these, yet the Giant Sable is confined to a small, definitely marked territory.

I wanted a group of these sables for the Philadelphia Academy of Natural Science but Angola on the west coast seemed a long way from Mombassa on the east coast. My knowledge of our destination was sketchy and did not embrace much more than that Angola was a Portuguese penal colony where the importation of guns was rigidly frowned upon and that many experienced hunters had been disappointed in their search there for Giant Sable.

I decided to cut across Africa from east to west along the old trade route over which so much "white and black ivory" had been brought to the coast during the last century. The railroad from Dar-es-Salaam in Tanganyika closely followed this trail, touching the old Arab strongholds of Kilossa and Tabora, towns built by the slave dealers to secure their line of communication from the great lakes of Central Africa to the coast.

This route awakened other memories on its span toward Lake Tanganyika. Just out of Tabora at Kivihara, my boyhood heroes, Stanley and Livingstone, lived together in 1872. Near the end of the tracks at Ujiji, on Lake Tanganyika, stands the historical mango tree under which they had met in 1871. Not far off from Kivihara is the pass between two hills where these great explorers parted. Furthermore I wanted to travel this route before the coming of the tourist procession, which now follows Thos. Cook & Sons from Cape to Cairo, had deflected its annual march and worn thin the romance still lingering over the old ivory and slave route, hallowed by historical memories.

At Kigoma, on Lake Tanganyika, began the tedious business of clearing our guns through the customs, so regularly to be repeated from there on through the Belgian Congo and Portuguese Angola. Customs formalities can be complied with in this free port, granted to the Belgians under the Treaty of Versailles.

With the help of a letter from ex-Governor General Lippens of the Congo, plus colossal patience and no little persuasion, we complied with all formalities and boarded the steamer which was to carry us and our thirty-three pieces of luggage across the lake to the Belgian Congo.

The S. S. Liemba, a trim little vessel built by the Germans before the war, sunk in the lake at the end of hostilities and finally raised and refitted by the British, sailed the eighty miles between Kigoma and Albertsville during the night. Amusing as it may seem, Bowen and I had to dine on deck because no one was admitted to the dining saloon without conventional dinner clothes, boiled shirt and all. My companion's pride smarted under this social restriction in the middle of Africa, but by dawn the prospect of innumerable birds to be studied beyond the Belgian lake port had soothed his resentment.

At Albertsville, District Commissioner Raffaele Caroli met us on the dock. Standing by him was a gang of convicts chained together by the neck, waiting to porter our luggage to the hotel. This friendly beginning, unfortunately, did not prevent the immigration authorities from nagging us all day with demands for our life histories before we obtained permits to carry arms. Their determination, despite our entreaties, to deface the stock of every gun by stamping registration numbers into the wood with metal discs was heart rending, and their charge of fifty francs per gun nearly broke our pocket books. However, a "Sundowner" and an excellent dinner at Commissioner Caroli's home brought our first day in the Belgian Congo to a pleasant close.

From there we rode 190 miles further by rail to Kabalo, through a country well wooded and clear of underbrush. Part of the time we followed the valley of the Lukuga River, through which Lake Tanganyika periodically empties. At Kabalo we were to board the S. S. Louis Cousin.

This steamer hove in sight about eight that evening, coming up the Lualaba River, but it took some hours to offload the cargo, including among other things, forty elephant tusks, not one of them exceeding twenty pounds in weight. The slowness of this offloading tried our patience. We were eager to shove off from Kabalo which comprised one brick railroad station, two tin roofed stores, two whitewashed residences of white railroad officials, a small native village, and, presumably, an invisible jail, for the usual gang of prisoners chained to each other by the neck, came down to the wharf to unload mail. Shortly after ten we settled aboard and protected by our mosquito nets, were soon asleep. Before daylight, the S.S. Louis Cousin started up the Lualaba. At this spot the river, which is really the upper Congo, is about two hundred yards wide and eight to ten feet deep at this August season of low water. We expected to sit many hours on sandbars before we arrived at Bukama, three hundred and fifty miles up the river.

A fringe of palms and mimosa trees lined the banks and out beyond, the country was better wooded than any part I had seen, except the slopes of Mt. Kenya. Frequently we noticed large brick buildings called Missions which were expensive churches and spacious enough to grace small cities rather than the measly native villages they dominated. They represented years of labor by the natives.

All along the river we saw visible signs of what the missionaries had accomplished. The bank of the Lualaba looked more like a Louisiana levee than a stream in the heart of the Congo. The clergy had tried to teach the natives modesty by dressing them up in tattered European clothes. It was not material to the negro mind that they frequently wore their skirts or trousers tied around their necks to keep them out of the way.

The captain, a young Belgian about thirty-two, had his little racket. Travellers paid the steamship company for passage only. The steward arranged to provide them with food for an agreed amount. This explained why at evening the captain frequently stopped the ship near the shore to shoot antelope. He succeeded mainly in crippling these animals. A worse marksman I never have seen. At one stop he fired seventeen shots, crippling five antelope and killing two females. A little later, another fusilade wounded several more animals, only one of which the "boys" drove out of the reeds to within twenty yards of the gallant captain's rifle. Then, with three more shots, he managed to kill the crippled antelope. This animal was also a female.

This nauseating business of crippling numerous animals produced meat for the steward, for which passengers paid. The captain of the ship was reimbursed by the steward with more ammunition to cripple more animals, none of which were followed up.

The first day out, we nosed through a huge papyrus swamp. Crocodiles were the main diversion, although the astounding variety of birds provided a never-ending source of interest. Open-billed storks in enormous numbers literally covered the sand bars. On our approach they rose in clouds, then swarmed into every available tree along the banks. We saw numerous other birds such as cormorants, darters, river eagles and geese, but these open-billed storks impressed us as being the most spectacular in this fascinating panorama of African river bird life. The second day's scenery was low lying swamp country through which the river twisted and turned, running straight for never more than a hundred yards at a time. The few native villages scattered along our tortuous route smelt to high heaven of fish refuse.

The waters of the upper Lualaba were now too low to float the S.S. Louis Cousin any further so a smaller paddle wheel steamer splashed alongside. We hustled aboard with our luggage, everyone trying to squeeze onto the bridge, the only spot on the boat that, because of its awning, offered even the suggestion of shade. The crowding promised to be more uncomfortable than the sun, so two of us climbed to the top of the pilot house. There we set up the Akeley camera in hopes of getting some good bird pictures, despite the little ship's great vibration.

After a long, scorching day, while the sun baked us as thoroughly as human flesh can be baked and still live, and sandbars retarded us as much as they could, sunset marked our arrival at a terrible place called Bukama. If Bukama had any place for us to sleep the Administrateur, who met us on instructions from the Governor General, was too drunk to recollect where it was. Finally we located a hotel where we could sleep in a room with six others. The Greek proprietor conjured up some food that actually cheered us. However, Bukama did have one big thing in its favor. It was the end of our first march toward Angola.

Next day I left for Elizabethville. The train was hours late and while we were waiting the Administrateur again became so drunk he could barely stagger. It was fortunate that he had, earlier in the day, ordered a chain of prisoners to carry our luggage to the station. While I went ahead to arrange the detail of the Angola trip, Bowen remained at Bukama despite its ugliness, because, he said, it looked like good bird country. We planned to meet in Tshilongo a week later.

Some days later I arranged to motor from Elizabethville, via Tshilongo, to Delolo Gare on the Angola frontier. I had engaged a car to arrive at six in the morning. At eight, I was still sitting on top of my luggage in front of the hotel. Then I went looking for the garage man. At ten, I was told it would surely be ready by eleven. At one, to my increasing rage, I was told absolutely without fail it would be ready at four.

At two I called on the director of the railroad and poured forth my troubles. He offered to run me to Tshilongo on the railroad in his private car. At Tshilongo he promised to get me a motor car for the rest of the way. So at six that evening when the local garage representative came to tell me that my long delayed car was finally ready, I had the exquisite pleasure of telling him to go to hell.

The Director's private car had been built for the King and Queen of the Belgians when in 1928 they had come to open the new railway connecting Port Francqui with Bukama. As we rolled along toward Tshilongo, I awakened to the fact that I was drinking my whisky and soda sitting on the Queen's couch. A large gilt plaque on the wall informed me of this. The glamour of royalty haunted my bed, for it, too, was the Queen's. Certainly it was not made for the tall King Albert whose height exceeded mine. If posterity ever tells that I once slept in the bed of the Queen of the Belgians, it will lie, for I never slept a wink. The royal bed was too short to stretch out in and too narrow to double up in.

But before we reached Tshilongo a good breakfast of papayas and scrambled eggs ironed out my spirits. When we arrived at the station, the woeful sight of Bowen, huddled on top of his luggage, made me, by comparison, seem like a pampered son. He had been dumped off his train at midnight, and finding no hotel in the little town, had slept by the track and gone without breakfast. My description of breakfast in the royal coach did not improve his disposition.

Three hours later our motor car arrived and by lunch time we were at Musonoi. This little village had one store and a scattering of native huts, but its future appeared assured. The Union Minière had opened several mines nearby. However, Musonoi's future did not provide us with a very satisfactory lunch.

During the next two days we traveled through an uninteresting country covered with scrubby timber that cut off all the view. Hunting here was a thing of the past. In a distance of over two hundred miles we saw only one antelope although this country had once fairly swarmed with game. It had all been shot out to provide meat for the Katanga miners.

Several times during the day's progress we had ferried across rivers on floats buoyed up by four or five dugout canoes. We regarded them with grave doubt, wondering if our heavy car would ever reach the other side. The floors were made of poles fastened to the canoes with strips of bark. The native ferrymen took the place of local newspapers and kept the gossip of the countryside in circulation. Any accidents that happened on their uncertain ferries threw them into a frenzy of jubilation.

Some of the bridges we had to cross were just as

exciting as the flimsy ferries. One of them, with a span of forty meters, did not have a single nail in it. It was fifty feet high at one point where it swayed alarmingly as the dry weather had loosened the bark strips that held it together. However, it did not fall and we reached the other side.

We covered the remaining hundred and ten miles to Delolo Gare on the frontier. In the morning we began the gruelling business of getting our guns out of the Belgian Customs and of searching for our permit to shoot Giant Sable in Angola. Although that important document was supposed to be at the border awaiting us, it was nowhere to be found. Therefore, more worried every minute over its non-appearance, we crossed the Luano River into Angola and drove eight miles into the town of Teixeira de Sousa in search of Major Torre de Valle who was reported to have our elusive permit.

We found the Major easily enough, but he had never so much as heard of us and of course knew nothing about our permit. But after we had established our identity, he did take us to the Customs and started the elaborate procedure of entering our guns into Angola.

We had heard enough about this business to leave our guns behind in Belgian territory while negotiations went on. Angola being a penal colony, it is a

difficult matter to get guns across the border. We had
friends who, after landing in the country, had spent
months trying to get their guns back from the Portuguese officials. In some cases nine months had passed
in negotiation. So we felt much more comfortable
discussing the business knowing our guns were safe
across the river in the Congo.

We had made a fair start in our conversation about
the guns, when by some lucky flash of memory, one
of the Customs officials recalled having seen a telegram with my name on it. A diligent search unearthed
a message from the Governor General instructing the
border officials to give us every facility and to grant us
free entry. This telegram was dated early in June.
The gun business was immediately settled and Bowen
started back to Delolo. I waited to see the Governor
of the Province who was expected on the incoming
train. I hoped that he might know something about
our permit to shoot the Giant Sable.

I received a very formal presentation to the Governor and then broached the subject. Yes, indeed, he
had been advised we were coming. Yes, indeed, he
had heard that we were to have a permit. But where
that permit might be, I knew as well as he.

I was disconsolate. And moreover, where was my
friend Evans who had promised to meet us at the
border, arrange our safari and select our Sable terri-

tory. I didn't even know where he expected us to leave the train. Returning to Delolo Gare I met Bowen also full of grief. In fact, he was in a panic. He was unable to buy railway tickets for us because the station master would accept no money except Angolars, the monetary unit of Angola. We had only dollars, sterling and Belgian francs and, of course, didn't have any Angolars. So we went to bed far from happy.

However, by train time the next morning I had with difficulty located enough of the accursed Angolars to start us on our journey. So gathering a flock of porters, we moved our luggage across the river, which forms the boundary between Angola and the Congo. That was where our train started, because the Belgai and the Portuguese could not decide on which side the Custom House should be located. It will probably take them years to agree.

On the other side we looked up Major de Valle again and he rejoiced to inform us that our shooting permit had arrived by mail. But most unfortunately, he had left his office in such a hurry to catch the train that he had forgotten to bring it along. But, of course, there was always the possibility that if we talked nicely to the conductor of the train, he might be persuaded to hold up the train at Teixeira de Sousa long enough for the Major to send to his office for the

document. So we treated the conductor to much unc-
tuous conversation and an equal amount of bribery.
The train waited. The permit was sent for. It arrived
just as the conductor's impatience over the unexpectedly long wait was about to demand further pleas-
antries.

We tore open the precious document. It was not a
permit to shoot a group of five sable. It was a permit
to shoot just two. We had taken this long trip across
Africa to get a group of five Giant Sable. Two, of
course, would not make a group. We were mad clear
through.

To add insult to injury, there was no word from
Evans. But again Major de Valle had a suggestion.
It was to get off at a station grandly named Villa
General Machado, where we were scheduled to arrive
the following morning.

Just before we had pulled out, the Governor of the
District of Moxico, His Excellency Vasco Lopes
Alves, boarded the train. Over glasses of beer, his
Excellency proved a sympathetic listener to our la-
ment about only two sable. As he was returning to the
Capital at Villa Sousa, we figured his good offices
might be of help to us in preparing telegrams to the
Governor General, and in fact every other official of
any influence in Angola who might get the additional
licenses.

At nine-forty next morning we arrived at the town which appeared on the maps as Camacupa, but which had recently been rechristened Villa General Machado. Our hearts went right down to our boots when we did not find Evans waiting for us. For some hours we rushed about sending telegrams to every place Evans might have been. Finally word came back that he expected to arrive late that night by motor.

We found an hotel. Its sign was the only word in town we could read. But as the proprietor spoke nothing but Portuguese, he led us to the store of Santos Cunha & Co., where we finally got our thoughts over to a clerk who, at least, had heard of the French language. He trotted us around to meet the Chef de Posto who had received a letter about us from the Governor. After lunch, we drove out to the Quanza River, twenty-one miles away. We stood high on the river bank in the native village of Chouzo. Looking out over the flats, we saw a low range of hills covered with brush. That spot was the haunt of the Giant Sable. It was the "promised land" to us, for it was the only place in the world where this rare and magnificent antelope could be found.

Chouzo is one of the largest villages of the Luimbi tribe. These natives are not famous for their industry nor do their women go in for beauty, but the men do well enough as porters and trackers and that was our main concern. The village, like all Angolan native villages, was set in a grove of mulemba trees which towered above the surrounding scrub. The huts of the chief and his three wives were encircled by a stockade of thick twelve-foot posts, with only one doorway, always securely fastened at night. The youngest wife was really the only good looking native woman we saw in Angola, which may explain both her dominance over her husband and his other wives, and also the securely fastened door after sunset. This black beauty was well known to the Portuguese officials who had dubbed her Mussolina.

To our huge relief, Evans arrived during the night. The next day we transported a load of food and gear to the Quanza River in his one-ton truck. The road was perfect, like most of the roads in Angola. Native labor at practically no cost and a rigid restriction against the traffic of native oxcarts seems to be the road policy. The results, so far as the visitor is concerned, are agreeable.

At Chouzo, Bowen and I shook out our camp and settled for the night. Evans and the Chef de Posto who had been riding with us, went back to Camacupa to get another load of our stuff. Before leaving us, however, the Chef de Posto held an impromptu court to try a native belle accused of a meandering taste in local gentlemen. Her husband's annoyance was caused not by her itinerant infidelity, but because she was in the habit of working in the corn field of her temporary lovers. His own corn fields needed *all* her working hours.

In the morning, with large safety pins and gaudy beads, we bribed the villagers to pose for our cameras. The natives were so obliging that we asked the Chef to stage a dance. The beating of drums and the slow circular thudding of seventy men, women and children was going splendidly until the arrival of Evans and his truck load of fuba (corn meal) and equipment broke up native concentration on rhythmic self-expression.

From the dancers and hangers-on we selected fifty-nine natives to serve as porters and assigned each one his load. Generally, each load weighed about thirty kilos (sixty-six pounds) but a few ran as heavy as seventy-five pounds. Our safari began the ferrying of the Quanza. It took over an hour to get all our porters and equipment to the other bank, during which time an ugly looking thunder storm kept coming nearer. The storm broke, drenching us, but we continued on for seven miles. For the most part we had followed native paths which, after years of use, were worn smooth and cut several inches deep into the soil. As the native places one foot directly in front of the other, the paths were only about six inches wide.

We were constantly tripping over our feet. We halted near a native village where the babbling porters assured us there were plenty of sable. The village chief immediately called and invited me to go with him at once to see the great number of sable just around the next tree. I had a walk and saw trees. That was all.

By daylight we were out again with eight native guides. But by eleven we returned to camp having seen no more of our sable than some fresh tracks. We did see three reedbuck, two duikers and two oribi.

The range of the Giant Sable antelope lies between the Loando and the Quanza Rivers, although a few specimens have been killed north of the Loando. Some have been seen southeast of the railroad where it crosses the Quanza, but, practically speaking, they are confined to this narrow strip of country one hundred miles long by about thirty miles wide. This animal was discovered by H. F. Varian, chief engineer of Benguella Railroad, in 1913. He had thereby solved an old mystery of a single horn in the museum at Florence measuring sixty-one inches long, or a foot longer than the best sable ever shot. Naturalists had puzzled for many years as to what animal could have carried this magnificent trophy. The Giant Sable differs from the ordinary sable of Rhodesia and Tanganyika principally in its size, facial markings, and the tremendous sweep of its horns, which approximate five feet in length.

The sable range is fairly level, with only gently rolling hills. It is covered with a dense growth of small trees which seldom exceed thirty feet in height. The quinsolle bush with its jasminelike flower and the chinbimburee plant, of which these sable are particularly fond, grow in profusion in this area. A heavy carpet of rank grass is burned off each year by the natives, but isolated patches which had escaped the fire showed that it stood four to six feet in height, which made hunting practically impossible until after it had been burned. When we first arrived the trees were for the most part bare of leaves, but, with the first rains in early October, they burst into full foliage, forming a screen which cut off our vision at not more than twenty-five or thirty yards. Our experience showed that the only time it is feasible to hunt in this country is after the grass has been burned off, say the first part of August, and before the rains have brought the trees into full leaf about October 1st.

Scarcity of sable signs induced us to move our camp six miles further up the backbone of the country between the Quanza and Loando Rivers. The next morning, two hours after daylight, we saw our first herd of sable.

They stood in thick bush. At first we could make

out their shadowy forms only with great difficulty. But as they moved about, crossing small openings, we discerned cows, young bulls and calves. There seemed to be twelve in the herd. Finally, the herd bull walked into view not more than eighty yards from where we stood. He looked coal black. His horns seemed tremendous.

Through the glasses, however, they did not seem so long. While I was trying to decide whether or not they measured the minimum shootable length of fifty inches, the herd caught our scent. Off they started. We followed their clearly marked track.

Just as we came into an open meadow I saw a roan antelope quietly feeding. It was a good bull and instantly I decided I would rather be certain of a good roan than take my chances on a poor sable. So, after some very bad shooting on my part, he fell.

Returning to camp I shot so badly at an oribi that I began to wonder if my gun needed targeting. Later, I found that it shot four feet to the left at a hundred yards. So we spent our first afternoon in camp resighting our guns and skinning out the head of the roan. During the rest of our Angola hunting, meat was hard to get, because this country seemed relatively destitute of game. It took a lot of meat to feed sixty men.

The following days dragged out in long hours of

tramping through monotonous bush where everything looked just like everything else. Not an outstanding hill or a rock or a stream broke the tiresome
repetition. Sometimes we could see about seventy-five
yards ahead through the scrub, but more often our
vision ended at thirty yards with a gray green wall of
trees. Once, to our immense relief, we mounted a hill
of sufficient elevation to give us a view of our surroundings.

From the summit, we saw country rolling away in
a series of horizons toward the Loando River in the
north. I counted no less than eight different rises
ranging in color from the gray green of the fore-
ground to misty blue on the farthest horizon. They
were all splashed with purple shadows from clouds
floating high above them.

I went down to Bowen's camp at Chouzo one afternoon, not so much to disturb his bird hunting as to do
something to hasten the extra license. I found the
Chef de Posto encamped there surrounded by his wife
and a flock of relatives. The Chef, himself, was undeniably white, about forty, and excellently built.
His wife was undeniably Portuguese but not so white.
But the relatives of the collateral branches ranged in
color from that of cream to that of black coffee. Of
course, the Portuguese do not draw the color line
sharply, especially in the colonies, so after four hun-

dred years of occupation of this colony the native darkness has in numberless cases gone lighter.

The Chef's family luncheon party was lively. He himself had come on ahead to collect the hut taxes from the natives and his family followed in an amazing procession of broken down automobiles. Musical instruments, liquor, a conglomeration of codfish in oil, cabbage soup, red wine and brave drunkenness made up the fiesta.

Just before dark the Chef's family rattled off to where they came from and the native chief got up a dance for our edification. The firelight flickered over the naked black bodies as they swayed to the tom-tomed rhythm. Bowen tried to teach the chief's wife, Mussolina, how to dance a fox trot. Without warning them, I took a flashlight photograph. That broke up the show.

In the morning, after a leisurely breakfast, we started forth on a lechwe hunt, guests of the Chef de Posto. We crossed to the farther side of the Quanza with forty-three beaters and there found three hammocks suspended from poles waiting our pleasure. I refused to go hunting in a hammock. In fact, I even insisted upon carrying my own gun. My rudeness nearly wrecked the hunt.

When we reached the marshes I saw a lechwe slip into cover seventy-five yards ahead of us. I fired a hit, and the lechwe left a blood trail for fully two miles, running in practically a complete circle before I could get in a finishing shot. The kill was made just twenty yards from where I first fired.

By this time we were assured the beaters had hundreds of lechwe and sitatunga headed our way. The Portuguese were literally trembling with excitement over the prospect of so much easy slaying. However, only one tiny lechwe doe appeared. I refused to shoot it. My first lechwe measured twenty-two and one-half inches, fully three inches longer than any other so far recorded in Angola.

The next day I drove to Camacupa to get more fuba. There I was offered two sable heads for 150 Angolars each. The strict protection of the Giant Sable seemed a myth. Only against foreign sportsmen were they protected. The Portuguese residents killed them wholesale and sold the heads. In fact, subsequently, I was offered any number of heads I cared to buy, and I heard several Portuguese brag of killing ten sable in a month. At that rate, this magnificent animal will soon be extinct.

On the 29th of September my special permit to shoot five sable arrived. This long awaited document had been telegraphed from Loando on the 21st of September, and had arrived in eight days. I could have walked the distance in the same time. Instead I had been sitting around watching natives brawl, Portuguese overeat and my own patience grow thinner. And, of course, every day brought us nearer the beginning of the Angola rainy season.

Within an hour, I was on the trail with two Portuguese hunters, Senhor Brito and Senhor Cavallo. We used only twelve porters and carried only absolutely necessary equipment. We camped that night on the Luaco River and started hunting at once, but did not see a single fresh track.

Next morning, between six and ten we plodded hopefully, but not one fresh track did we find. If my feet had not been so blistered and if the jiggers had not been so friendly, I should have moved camp that night. The heat was terrific. It rained too. We were not very happy.

Sitting in the rain, digging out jiggers, unable to talk to my Portuguese hunters who spoke no tongue but their own, was a woeful business. However, my tent boy, one Antonio, understood just about a score of English words. Strenuously I tried to explain to him that I needed one big bull, one immature bull, two cows and one calf to complete my group. After an hour's conversation this translated as follows: "One man, one little boy, two girls, and one children." I decided to let it go at that, only hoping we could get them, by any name.

It began to rain and kept it up all through that mournful night. We, of course, feared the real rains were upon us for that would mean the end of our sable hunt. Fresh meat for camp had given out and we ate potato soup and tapioca pudding for three consecutive meals to the drip of rain.

In the morning I killed a duiker and Senhor Brito got a bush pig, so we had meat. Then we started tracking sable. We found the fresh tracks of a herd, but, after two hours, lost them in rocky ground. Extremely weary and decidedly footsore I returned to camp by noon to find both my Portuguese hunters garrulous about all the sable they had seen near the camp. But neither had bothered to shoot any. In the afternoon, my hunt netted me a Warener lizard. It darted out of a clump of brush and dashed away through the grass with amazing speed. However, it ran up a tree, so I was able to shoot it with a solid Springfield bullet. The natives told fanciful tales of this Warener lizard, claiming that it crept up on a sleeping person and stopped up both his nostrils with its forked tongue. When the victim had been smothered to death, the lizard devoured him. Our specimen measured sixty-two inches in length. I saw in it the makings of a fine pair of shoes for my daughter.

The unrelieved sameness of this country began to wear on my nerves. Not one landmark stood out, and when the sun was clouded as it was much of the time, getting lost or "bushed" was the easiest possible thing to do. Hunting under such conditions really degenerated into wandering about, hoping to stumble on sable. Occasionally we found fresh tracks, but invariably lost them in the mass of dead leaves and new grass. Our native trackers were certainly inferior to East Coasters, but I must confess that even they saw many more tracks than I, and could also read into those tracks far more information about the elusive sable. Furthermore, once the decision to give up our aimless wandering was made, these natives could strike a perfectly straight line for camp, which was more than I could do even with the aid of my compass.

Each day we saw fewer tracks and the natives roundabout told us that as the rainy season approached, sable moved to higher ground. Therefore, well convinced that our game had moved out of the country along the Luasco River we set out toward Samatembo on the Coluando River. On the way to our new camp I was persuaded to try riding in a teepoy or hammock. But the carriers groaned and grunted so under my weight, that I abandoned this after ten minutes and walked. I subsequently discovered that their groans and grunts were in the nature of a chant and all my sympathy had been wasted.

Before daylight the Samatembo camp received its

baptism of rain that lasted until noon. So we pushed on in an effort to get out of the district where the heavy rains had commenced. The two Portuguese and I hunted ahead while the boys packed up. At four, by agreement, we all met at a native village called Sachimbanze.

While we were pitching camp the village chief arrived, bearing the usual gift of a chicken and a bowl of rice. When my boys saw him approach, they hustled out a chair so that I might receive him in approved style. That style seemed to be as follows. You pretend to ignore his approach even when he finally stands directly before you flanked by several henchmen. Ultimately, you do acknowledge his repeated salutations and send a boy forward to accept his gifts. Then, during the ensuing palaver and his earnest repetition that the warmth of his heart is for you, you look painfully bored. The big moment of the ceremony is when you coldly announce that you will judge his statements by the number of sable his hunters locate for you.

Meanwhile he grows visibly nervous lest you are not going to give him a present and you go on letting him grow more nervous just as long as you can stand having him near you. You nod to your boy. He brings out a roll of cloth. You measure off four meters. Then with a magnificent gesture you order your boy to hand the four meters of cloth to the chief and to tell him that if his men locate sable you will be even more generous when you depart. If your mood is unusually liberal, the game provides that you inquire how many wives he has so that you may send each a pocket mirror or a string of beads.

Within the next few days we picked up the tracks of a herd. For three strenuous hours we followed these tracks across places where the sable had bedded down, through thick brush where they had stopped for a long feed and over channas which they had crossed in haste. After about seven miles of this tracking we found blades of grass, still wet, which had fallen from their mouths, and occasional dung, still steaming. Suddenly we heard a shot a few hundred yards ahead of us. We ran forward. There was my Portuguese Senhor Brito consoling himself on a miss.

It developed that he had come upon the herd from the opposite direction and had fired at six hundred yards. What was even more infuriating, was that the herd was not sable but roan. This fact convinced me that I could not tell the difference between roan and sable tracks. When Brito claimed he could, my disposition was not improved.

Having hunted this country thoroughly and conspicuously without success, we moved on to Cacunda, situated on the very top of the watershed between the

Photo by Prentiss N. Gray.

THE LUIMBI WITCH-DOCTOR COUNTERACTED THE SPELL
FOR TWO ANGOLARS — EQUIVALENT TO FIVE CENTS

Quanza and Loando Rivers. The country was some of the best I had ever seen, being strikingly like an English park. It consisted mainly of open channas through which you could see beneath the trees for at least a couple of hundred yards. But unfortunately, this beautiful hunting country suffered the same drawback as all ideal hunting grounds. The animals you are seeking seem to avoid places so pleasant for the hunter.

I was out at six the morning after we arrived, feeling on a hunch that my luckiest day in Africa had just dawned. It turned out to be the worst. Despite the fact that the morning fog filled the hollows and channas, we found a herd of sable before eight. I crawled up to within sixty yards of a good cow, just the lady for my museum group. I fired twice. I missed twice. At a hundred and fifty yards, I did hit her in the hind leg. She started off and we gave a long chase during which I fired three more shots. At eleven we lost the trail, so we had to abandon our chase. Snap shooting at running animals through dense bush was apparently one of the things I did not do so well.

I returned to camp angry and disgusted and heartsick. When my tent boy asked for two Angolars to pay the local medicine man to counteract the spell a neighboring medicine man must have cast over me, he got his two Angolars in a hurry. I was assured that for the money, the friendly medicine man would have sable antelope walking right into camp begging to be killed. I was ready to do anything to change my luck, for the camp was in the doldrums, murmuring because the boss could not find sable, and when he did, could not shoot them.

I hunted six hours next day and saw nothing but three duikers. Brito claimed to have shot up a herd of twenty-four sable and to have knocked down a cow and a bull. But evidently, he had forgotten to bring them in for he returned to camp empty handed.

Gloomy and exhausted, I went to sleep that night; but, with elegant perversity, the village natives had arranged a little get-together. The dancing began at sundown and gave promise of going on until sun up. Around ten I went over, determined to stop the racket. But I found myself tarrying, fascinated.

The dancers formed a large circle, with men on one side, women on the other, placing the drums on the outside. After the drums had been beaten for some time, the chanting commenced, first from the men, two of whom advanced with odd pacing, toward the center. Suddenly the women answered the chant and rushed forward, anklets clanking and voices raised, to drive back the two dancing males. Although this performance had been going on for hours, my order to stop raised a howl of protest.

But the Chief backed me up. He liked me. For days we had been receiving delegations from his village, all of them seeking medical care. The ills ran the gamut from tropical ulcers to pregnancy. My medical repertory consisted of applications or doses of permanganate of potash, mercurocrome and Epsom salts. All of these made a brave visible display and produced evident results. So, of course, the Chief wanted to prove his gratitude and disbanded his dancers. He went even further. He insisted that his favorite wife spend a couple of days with me. Most graciously I thanked him for such brotherly liberal mindedness, but refused. However, I presented the lady with a small mirror to prevent her taking offense. And of course, the mirror might explain to her why I was forced to decline her companionship.

Early morning hunting in this country was rather joyful. The sun was a red ball that just looked over the tops of the hills beyond the Loando. The woods, open enough underneath to make walking easy, were checkered with sunlight. The grass was freshly sprouted, but grown long enough to hide the charred stumps of last year's growth. Every tree was in full, vivid leaf, having lost nothing of its freshness. Pairs of pygmy geese would frequently rise from a reed bed around a pool in the woods.

Flowers seemed to grow everywhere in the green

shade of the woods. A delicate pink lily bloomed in prodigal abundance. Sometimes there were deep purple lilies with a splash of yellow in their hearts. Morning glories bloomed in the shade and in the open channas there were patches of crinum. These plants bore a dozen blooms on their single stalks; flowers that were pure white with a magenta stripe down the length of each petal.

But by noon, the insects would grow so pestiferous that life seemed a bit less joyous. Six hours of fast walking with natives who never stroll produced weary feet and hunger. The sun grew violent and the heat relentless through thin trees, none of them more than thirty feet in height and so, unable to cast dense shade. Crossing the open channas became a nightmare for there the sun beat down squarely on our heads. We were hemmed in on all sides by a wall of green. Our eyes grew tired from straining to pierce this wall for game. Fifty yards were the farthest we could see. The lush green beneath our feet became hateful for it hid the sable tracks we might have followed. Frequently we trudged near pools, only to find stagnant water. Myriad swarms of tiny green insects swished from the bushes against our faces. We could not breathe without inhaling them. So we held our breath until past the bushes. We became desperately footsore, hungry and thirsty. There seemed to be

absolutely no game. At last we staggered into camp,
pulled off our boots and crawled under mosquito nets.
After a rest there was a sundowner. Then food. At
last in the soft, short twilight you might rejoice in
the sight of the red ball of sun sinking behind the
tops of the hills beyond the Quanza.

The natives of Angola proved themselves to be
better at conversation than at tracking. Ask them the
simplest question such as "Have we any sugar left?"
and they would consume half an hour answering.
Propound a debatable question such as "Where shall
we hunt in the morning?" and they would argue it
far into the night and in the morning give this kind
of answer. "Tracks, freshly made, have been seen two
hours walk to both north and east. West of us is a
splendid feeding ground and the villagers claim that
yesterday, when hunting honey to the south, they saw
a big bunch of Sumba Coloco." Then you say, "Well,
under those circumstances, there is, of course, nothing
to do but go this way, and you start off in the direction
you happen to be facing."

My tent boy, Antonio, was the best conversationalist
in camp. He poured out so much language I decided
to throw him out of camp. But he pleaded frantically
to stay. I gave him the alternative of making a fool
of himself by mounting a petrol box and there getting
all his conversation off his chest at one time by talk-

ing steadily for an hour to the vacant air. He agreed. An hour later I went out to tell him his punishment time was up. I found him shouting at the top of his lungs while seated before him were not only all the camp boys, but also most of the villagers. They were spellbound to a man. Antonio begged me to allow him to continue, for this had turned out to be his day.

After three weeks the big moment arrived. I was puzzling out some sable tracks when my gun bearer touched my arm. He whispered the magic word, "Sumba Coloco," (the native name for Giant Sable).

The animal stood so still beside a tree that I did not see him for a second. The first thing I made out was two splashes of white on his face. Then his large, jet black body. When he wheeled to run I saw the majestic sweep of his horns. I fired. But he dashed away. I thought I had missed until I found a blood spot on the leaves. Then we knew we still had a chance of seeing that magnificent head again.

We tracked him over difficult stony ground and, after a few hundred yards, jumped him again. I had shot him in the shoulder, breaking it. Nevertheless, he seemed able to run as fast on three legs as on four, and his breathing was unimpaired. We manoeuvered for a clear view. Then with the greatest care, I fired again. This shot finished him. The horns measured sixty-one and a quarter inches in length; twelve inches in circumference at the base. I had travelled half way around the world for such a trophy. Jubilantly we measured, photographed and skinned him out, preparing him for his new habitat in Philadelphia at the Academy of Natural Sciences. The fresh scars on his body lead us to conclude that he had been driven out of the herd recently in a fight with a younger bull.

After skinning our bull, we started back to camp because it was almost ten and we did not expect to see any more sable at so late an hour. However, luck was prodigal that morning and in a little while we discovered a herd feeding in an open parklike space which in Angola is called a channa. We counted ten of them, eight cows, one calf and a grand old black bull.

I studied his horns through the glasses. As accurately as I could make out, they were nearly as large as those of the huge bull I had just killed. Very quietly, I slipped around him through the woods for a quarter of a mile until I had the wind right and had approached within two hundred and forty yards. That seemed about as near as I dared crawl without startling him. I had to wait for my shot. The cows and especially the calf, all a rich reddish brown, kept him covered while they peacefully fed along. They fed in a strung out formation and the bull was on the farther side. The sable bulls, like so many other bulls among herds of African game, stay offside, leaving the leadership to the cows. They attend to the breeding and fighting and are not interested in other herd affairs. Finally, between the cows, the bull offered a clear shot. I fired twice, hitting him both times. On the second shot, he bolted for a small clump of trees in the middle of the channa.

We ran hard parallel to him, being careful to keep to leeward of him. We crept up to where we thought he had fallen. There he was, down and certainly dying. I signalled to my gun boy that we would not shoot him up any more. But so erect did the bull hold his head and so freely did he keep moving it, that I decided to try a finishing shot. It ploughed into his neck but instead of finishing him, it got him to his feet and off like a streak of lightning toward the timber. I hit him twice more before he could reach the protecting woods. He crumpled and when we came up to him he was dead.

Measuring him carefully, we found his horns only two inches less than those of the first bull killed that morning. They were fifty-nine inches long and ten and a quarter inches at the base.

The next excitement was the noisy arrival of the chief of a nearby village who had agreed, but failed, to be at our camp at five-thirty to guide me on the hunt. With several followers, he rushed up just as I had finished measuring the second bull to tell me that he and his men had deliberately driven this bull across my path so I could shoot him. Of course it was all utter nonsense as the herd, when we first saw it, was peacefully feeding and was not being driven any place. As this chief had hunted with us for two days when I refused to shoot everything that jumped up, he had probably decided to go off on a honey-search of his own. This he had been doing when he heard my shot, and was greatly incensed when I indicated that his tale was a lie and that he was not entitled to any of the sable meat.

Into that one day were crowded much luck and excitement but we made up for it by the days of monotony that followed while we tried to complete our group. I had ample time to study the natives of our safari. On this Angola hunt, native porters carried everything on their heads. There were no trucks, of course, and it took me back to the days of old time African hunting when native backs did all the hauling. We had fifty-nine porters, a number which constantly astonished me. As soon as they arrived in camp, they set about building grass huts for themselves. As a result, it looked as though our tent was the center of a permanent African village.

The natives were all geniuses in inventing minor troubles. They were in constant want of something. They all went in for an epidemic of minor ills that required curing on the spot. Their clothes, what they had of them, were ever in need of needle and thread. And just for good measure they fought among themselves from morning until night like a horde of ill-tempered children. Their favorite pastime was stealing fuba and meat from each other. As a result, our camp in the famous silences of Africa seemed always a noisy bedlam.

Evans knew how to handle them and, while he was with me, I let him run the show his way. Each boy received two cupfuls of fuba a day. But the natives from the nearby villages would steal into camp and line up with our boys when mealtime arrived. Of course, it was difficult for us to recognize all our own. So, when there were seventy in line one day, Evans passed out the regulation fifty-nine rations, then stopped. Much howling and raging, but the next day our own men saw to it that no visitors cut them out of their food.

Their appetite for meat was gargantuan. On one checkup, these fifty-nine boys devoured twelve hundred pounds of fresh meat in three days beside their regular rations of fuba.

Several days after I had killed my sables, Evans went out on a hunt. I heard him shooting and prayed his shots were ploughing into a good sable which, for a number of years, he had been most anxious to kill.

An hour later, a runner came in for porters. But the porters carried in no sable; Evans had killed only a couple of moderate sized roan antelope for meat.

This small disappointment was just the prelude to my horror at discovering that the hair on my two sable hides was beginning to slip. By frantic working-in of very fine salt, after paring down the skin on the thick places, we stopped the threatened destruction of our trophies.

My experience in hunting sable was of course limited. But from what the Portuguese and the natives told me, I was convinced that my difficulty was general and that sable were as hard to kill as hartebeeste. They can take an amazing lot of lead. In the case of my two bulls, for example; if they had been any kind of American game, the first shots would have been quickly fatal. My second sable bull had traveled over half a mile after the first mortal shot, and another hundred yards after three more vital shots in him.

Looking back over my entire African hunt, I could recall only three instances when antelope dropped when hit. Those were a Grant's gazelle, a waterbuck and a dik dik. The others had all traveled from fifty to five hundred yards after being hit. This of course made little difference when I was hunting on the open plains or scattered bush of Kenya and Tanganyika,

because the animals could easily be followed by sight
or track.

When I shot the first sable, the small trees, not
over thirty feet in height, and quinsalle bushes, with
their jasmine-like flowers, were not yet covered with
leaves. But the first rains of October caused them to
burst into foliage. Our recent glimpses of sable had
been through dense green screens so we did not see the
entire animal. Only a dark mass would be visible, as
we drew down, through the sights. After a shot, the
screen would close as the animal dashed away, leaving
a barely visible trail. To pick out the tracks of the
wounded animal from the tracks of the herd was most
difficult. It began to look as if the only thing to do
was to wait until next August when the grass had been
burned again and the trees were bare of the obscuring
leaves. I did not intend to cripple animals we had no
hope of getting, or to kill several others which we
could never locate afterward.

We spent six more days of steady plodding through
the bush. Not finding one sign of sable, we were convinced that the season was too far advanced for
further hunting. We completed a sixty mile swing
through the country by moving our camp back to the
Luasco. Then, on that watershed, we made one more
effort, but we did not find a single track and returned
to Camacupa.

On the 19th of October, we left Camacupa, post-poning until the following year the hunt for the needed sable cows. A twenty-six hour rail trip gave us our first view of the Atlantic Ocean at Benguella. Our trans-African trip along the Livingstone Trail was complete. It seemed a fitting end to that long trail through the haunt of the sable, that friends had arranged for us to stay in the Lobito home of H. F. Varian, the discoverer of the Giant Sable.

Summary of trip across Africa

	Miles
Dar-es-Salaam to Kogoma (rail)	765
Kigoma — Albertville (Lake Steamer)	88
Albertville — Kabalo (rail)	190
Kabalo — Bukama (River steamer on Lualaba)	348
Bukama — Tshilongo (rail)	124
Tshilongo — Delolo Gare (auto)	335
Delolo Gare — Lobito (Benguella Railway)	830
Across Africa	2660

CHAPTER VI.

The Portage Route of the Gaspé

By HUGH CABOT

During the years between 1890 and 1900, in various perambulations which I made in the state of Maine and in New Brunswick, I frequently encountered, among the Indians, rumors to the effect that in times gone by the Indian tribes on the north shore of the St. Lawrence were in the habit of moving from that region to the coast of Maine and even to Massachusetts Bay. Such rumors were wholly unsubstantial and yet excited my curiosity. For the tribes living in western Quebec a ready route could be found from the St. Lawrence by way of tributaries of the Kennebec, but there were persistent rumors to the effect that tribes living in eastern Quebec as far east as the region of Seven Islands made this same trip. For them the route above indicated would have been long and hazardous, involving extensive navigation of the Gulf of St. Lawrence which might easily have proved a risky journey. For them, the obvious route would have been by way of the Bay of Chaleur had it not been for the inconvenient protrusion of the Gaspé

Peninsula. To cross the Gulf and round the eastern extremity of the Gaspé might readily have been a more serious business than they would have cared to undertake. To cross the Gaspé Peninsula involved negotiating the Shickshock Mountains, a range of no great height, but rather steep and rocky, occupying the whole back-bone of the Gaspé Peninsula. Most of the rivers in this region rise in this range and run either north or south to the St. Lawrence or to the Bay of Chaleur respectively. Once arrived in the Bay of Chaleur access to the rivers of Maine was very simple. By ascending the Restigouche to a point to the north of Baker Lake and thence passing to the west branch of the Penobscot, or to the point where the West Branch passes Moose Head Lake, they had ready access to the head waters of the Kennebec. Thus the difficulty appeared to reduce itself to the negotiation of the Gaspé Peninsula. In this connection it should be noted that the Indians of the Bay of Chaleur region are the Mic Macs. This tribe was apparently entirely distinct from the Indians of Maine and New Brunswick and also from the Montagnais of the north shore of the St. Lawrence. They have a very rich language not understood by the Montagnais, but I found that they understood and could translate Indian names in common use throughout the New England States.

145

I am told that there has been much controversy over their origin and recall a story attributed to the late Professor Agassiz when he was attending a scientific meeting where such questions were being discussed. It appeared that he was not vitally interested and fell asleep. Being called upon by the chairman for his opinion he rather suddenly heard the question, "Professor Agassiz, what do you believe to be the origin of the MicMacs?" He answered promptly, "Perfectly simple, Scotch-Irish." This opinion, though open to dispute, may perhaps be as good as any other. These Indians have a large reservation in the form of a Crown Grant, dating back at least some centuries, on the north shore of the Bay of Chaleur from the mouth of the Matapedia eastward along the shore of the Bay for more than fifty miles. Their chief settlement is at Cross Point near the head of the Bay. These data seemed important since I assumed that it would be from these Indians that I should be most likely to obtain information as to a possible portage route across the Peninsula.

I had for several years been travelling extensively in New Brunswick and Quebec with a member of that tribe known as Tom Germa, the most finished woods companion that it has been my good fortune to meet. His inquiries led nowhere and in 1903 I undertook a preliminary expedition to see whether or not there was a river which cut through the mountains and therefore became accessible from the south side.

For this purpose I ascended the Grand Cascapedia, a beautiful river, and readily navigable in Gaspé boats practically to its head. On this occasion I took with me a Frenchman of the inspiring name of Napoleon Bois who claimed to be familiar with the country. As might have been expected the allegation proved to be entirely false, and his capacity to do anything other than eat and sleep was of the smallest. Leaving the Grand Cascapedia where it divided into two small tributaries we readily reached the Shickshock Mountains and had no difficulty in climbing to the flat plateau on their top after a walk of about three days from the river. Travelling eastward along this plateau we soon came to a deep cut through which a river flowed from the south and we had reason to believe that this was the river known as the St. Anne emerging on the Gulf of the St. Lawrence at the little settlement St. Anne des Monts. It seemed likely that the head of this river lay in more or less close relation to the Little Cascapedia and that no great difficulty would be experienced in making a satisfactory portage route in that way. On that grassy plateau there was evidence that it had been inhabited by caribou in large numbers in the past as shown by many old horns that had been shed, but in several

147

days we only saw one small bunch of the animals, one of which, however, was a very large and very old specimen of the woodland caribou.

During the winter of 1905 and 1906 Tommy succeeded in finding in one of the settlements, considerably east of Cross Point, a very old Indian who told him the following story. He said that his father something like one hundred years before had gone up the Little Cascapedia and crossed over to a lake which evidently ran into the St. Lawrence. On this lake he met some Indians whose language he could not understand, and he came to the conclusion that they must have come from the north side of the Gulf. His father had apparently given him a fairly clear description of the lake and he volunteered to tell us how it might be reached. He pointed out what I knew to be true that navigation of the Little Cascapedia would be practically impossible because of natural log jams in its upper portion, the removal of which would be very difficult and time-consuming. He suggested that the best route would be to go up the Grand Cascapedia to a considerable hill known as Berry Mountain at which point would be found Berry Mountain Brook entering the river from the east. He said that by going up this brook one would find a small pond which had an outlet in both directions, namely westward to the Grand Cascapedia and eastward to the Little Cascapedia, that by following the brook to the eastward we should reach the Little Cascapedia well up toward the mountains, and that it would probably be more or less navigable up to the point where it reached the neighborhood of St. Anne Lake, assuming that the lake, of which he had heard, was in fact on the head of the St. Anne River. He told us very categorically that the place to leave the Little Cascapedia was at a point where a mountain with a double rocky peak lay directly north of the river, and that the alleged lake lay upon the right or easterly side of the mountains. This information seemed worth following up and likely to result at least in an amusing jaunt in the Peninsula. We could get practically no information in regard to the upper portion of the St. Anne River. The lower portion was leased as a salmon river, said at that time to be controlled by Mr. Charles Schwab but at a point some twenty miles from the mouth there was a considerable falls aggregating some forty or fifty feet which put an end to the salmon fishing, and consequently to the sporting interest in the river. From this it appeared to follow that there might be a good stretch of the upper St. Anne running through the Shickshock Mountains, probably with a considerable pitch and of quite unknown quality in regard to roughness.

The problem therefore involved obtaining a practicable canoe which should have unusual seaworthy qualities, carry sufficient provisions to partly supply two men for something like a month, and yet be sufficiently light to lend itself to a not inconsiderable amount of bushwhacking which was obviously involved. For this purpose I had built a 16 foot canoe much economizing weight by lowering the peak and stern and raising the gunwale in the midship section about 4 inches. It was not a thing of beauty, but as events proved, was a very capable little sea boat.

In this connection a somewhat amusing incident occurred. The boat having been duly shipped by express I wrote to Tom Germa asking him to see whether it had arrived. He wrote me through the medium of the padre at Cross Point that there was no canoe at Campbellton, the railroad point on the Bay of Chaleur directly across from Cross Point. However, I assumed that it would be there and in the early part of October went to Campbellton. Investigation of the freight house disclosed my canoe, but when inquiring of Tommy why he had had difficulty he replied, "Oh, dat not canoe, dat cockle shell." In other words he was entirely skeptical as to whether or not two more or less able-bodied men ought to undertake navigation of any river in such a craft. It may be noted at this point that his views in regard to it changed promptly and radically, later.

As the lower portion of the Grand Cascapedia involves steady poling against water of moderate strength, it seemed to me wise to take a Gaspé boat and an Indian to help us transport our outfit to the mouth of Berry Mountain Brook. Arriving at the river about ten o'clock on a raw, rainy day, it was suggested that Tommy take about 100 pounds of stuff in the little canoe and proceed up the river, the Indian and I to follow with the remainder. Being a person who always construed orders with perfect literalness, he did as he was told and disappeared. As the day was rainy no stop was made at lunch time, but about four o'clock Tommy was observed sitting on the shore in an attitude that suggested he thought proceedings might be properly discontinued for the day. When asked about the canoe, he said, "Oh, dat nothing, poling dat just fun. Grand little canoe."

Two days poling brought us to the mouth of Berry Mountain Brook, and having assorted our loads with, I think, excellent judgment by which Tommy carried the canoe and about 40 pounds, while I carried the balance, a start was made up Berry Mountain Brook. The going was neither better nor worse than was to be expected. Had it been my lot to carry the canoe, I should have spent most of my time butting it into trees and emitting language quite unfit to print. Tommy on the contrary wangled his way through the brush with surprising ease and night found us at the alleged pond described by the old Indian, which surprisingly enough proved to have two outlets, one of which led to the eastward and presumably to the Little Cascapedia.

From this double-vented mudhole, the outlet leading to the eastward was followed for another day of bushwacking and brought us to a good-sized stream corresponding in size and position to the upper part of the Little Cascapedia. The old Indian had suggested that this portion of the river was likely to be less obstructed with log jams than the lower portion, and on the following morning in a cold drizzling mixture of snow and rain a start was made up stream. It soon appeared that our informer's qualifications as a prophet were not great and that the river was much blocked with logs, requiring constant wading, hauling, unloading, and all of the inconveniences which go with attempts to navigate unnavigable waters. The pitch was not severe and we continued on at a poor rate of progress in intermittent squalls of rain and snow until about four o'clock when a satisfactory camping place was selected. As our diet had been a little restricted at least as far as meat was concerned, an attempt was made to pick up some grouse while Tommy was fixing camp. The chase, which was unsuccessful, led over a small hill and downward to-

ward the river evidently crossing a considerable ox-
bow of the stream. Having proceeded not more than
a mile, suspicious tracks were encountered which
proved to be our own and suggested that we had
spent the greater part of a perfectly good day in going about a mile in a straight line. This led to a re-
consideration of our plans with the result that we took
to the side-hill, bag and baggage, and were fortunate
enough to find some remnants of an old and reasonably passable trail following the river at no great distance. Following this for two days in which we made
perhaps fourteen miles we camped in the evening near
the river. A practice had been made of going out to
the river periodically to ascertain whether a sight
could be had of the two rocky peaks to which our Indian mentor had referred. On the following morning
on going out into the river, these peaks could be clearly seen lying at no great distance directly ahead. It
seemed reasonable to assume that we had followed
the river as far as was worth while and that it would
now turn sharply to the eastward without approaching any nearer to the mythical St. Anne Lake. It
therefore seemed wise to take a lunch and examine
the situation on the east side of these mountains with
the expectation of finding the lake, or at least evidences of the head waters of the St. Anne.

The day was fine, clear, cool, and stimulating. The

country, however, proved to be a large, quite flat, cedar swamp, than which there are few things less conducive to progress. At the time of crossing the river which could be readily waded, I noted that Tommy turned and looked carefully at the left or western shore and showed some reluctance to leave it, but true to his habit of giving no advice unless required he made no comment. By three o'clock in the afternoon we had apparently exhausted the possibilities of the cedar swamp with nothing to show for it, and a council of war seemed indicated. A dialogue somewhat as follows ensued. I pointed out that we had now reached a point almost directly east of the mountain referred to by the old Indian and therefore said, "We know that the lake must lie upon this side of the mountain if indeed there is any lake here at all."

Tommy: "No, we not know lake here. I not been here. Old Indian he say so. He not been here."

I then asked him point blank what he would do if he wanted to reach St. Anne Lake and he said, "Go back where we were in morning. Go west from old camp ground."

I asked him to what camp ground he referred and he replied, "Oh, old camp ground just above where we sleep las' night."

I suggested that I saw no camp ground. "Oh," he

said, "It growed up with brush and sprouts, but they camp there."

I said, "How long since you believe they were there?"

"Oh, hundred years — something like dat."

In short, at the time of crossing the river he had seen quite clearly that an area on the shore had been cleared and had now grown up with birch and other hard wood so that it was entirely obscure. On returning to the river, where we arrived about four o'clock, one could plainly see carved out upon the western shore between the considerable growth of spruce and pine, an area two or three hundred feet long grown up heavily with hard wood. Careful examination showed to my unpracticed eye no evidence that it had been used by human beings, but on this matter Tommy had no doubt. He said, "Oh, yes, this old camp ground. The lake lie this side not other side of mountain." In fact by proceeding in a northwesterly direction for less than a mile we reached a considerable lake which proved to be St. Anne Lake.

This illustrates to me the very interesting habit of mind of the hunting Indian who knows his own business but never feels required to give advice unless asked. He was perfectly willing to waste a whole day floundering around in the cedar swamp rather than intrude an opinion which ran counter to one which he knew I held, clearly as the result of quite insufficient evidence. On many other occasions he showed this same, as I think, very desirable, characteristic of minding his own business and assuming that I would mind mine.

St. Anne Lake proved to be a commonplace sheet of water somewhat oval, perhaps two miles in its longest diameter which was roughly north and south and a mile wide. From it, the Shickshock Mountains on both sides, could be readily seen and its outlet clearly led to the gorge which we had more or less definitely located the previous year. The next day was overcast and threatening rain so that we made no plan to move, but spent the morning in fishing. Our efforts were wholly futile, and we later learned that this river is entirely without fish above the falls. We were camped at the southern end of the lake in some fairly heavy spruce timber, and toward noon, having abandoned fishing as the rain was heavy and turning to snow, we set about the more important business of getting something to eat. During this performance a heavy wet snow driven by a strong northeasterly gale, developed and quite to my surprise a spruce tree, against which I was leaning in the attempt to fry over the fire, fetched away about four feet above my head. This was accompanied by the disappearance of other trees in the neighborhood, and it soon became evident that between the wet snow and the gale a blow-down of some proportions was taking place. At Tommy's suggestion all of the trees which could fall upon us were cut away, thus relieving us from the danger of being clubbed with a tree top. This having been satisfactorily accomplished however, it appeared quite impossible to keep a fire going in the young desert which we had created. But for this emergency Tommy was entirely prepared and proceeded to cut off some ten feet of the tops of six or eight spruce trees and banked them up behind and on the sides of the tent to form a wind screen. This worked beautifully except for a not inconsiderable tendency to draw the fire into the tent, which periodically during the balance of the day and night became moderately uninhabitable. The wind held through the night and every few minutes one could hear considerable trees on the ridges snap and break as a sort of staccato punctuation to the obligato of the gale. We afterward learned that this was a serious gale which did great damage along the coast of Newfoundland, Gaspé, and New Brunswick.

As there was nothing about St. Anne Lake which would tempt one to delay we made our way down the river for about one day's travelling, perhaps twenty to twenty-five miles, until we were squarely in the cut made by the river through the mountains. Thoughtlessly, as will presently appear, we camped upon the east bank since the other shore was steep and rocky. The next day was consumed in investigating the mountains on the west and a very moderate climb took us onto the same grassy plateau which we had reached the year before. The caribou seemed to be even more scarce, but we did succeed in killing a calf a few months old which fitted nicely into our somewhat monotonous diet. That night a tremendously heavy rain developed and at daylight we found ourselves in the interesting predicament of being on an island with considerable water in the brush around us and a roaring torrent between us and the canoe which we had carelessly left on the east shore. After moving to a safer spot and wasting a great deal of time in building a fire from wet wood, we faced the problem of getting in touch with our canoe. The river here was narrow and could be readily spanned by one of the fair sized spruce which grew close to the shore. One of these was cut and fell nicely in position but immediately was swept down by the stream and went down to bother us later as an obstruction. After moving up and down the shore and cutting about six trees, we finally got one which was anchored on our side by its own stump and on the other side by solid lodgement against the alder bushes. Though the water ran over this to the depth of some inches it made a passable bridge which enabled us to have

THE SHICKSHOCK MOUNTAINS

Photo by Prentiss N. Gray.

our camp, ourselves, and our canoe on the same side of the river. This phenomenon of rapidly rising water was one which we might very readily have foreseen since the Shickshock Mountains are pretty barren, with relatively little vegetation, and pour their waters very directly into any neighboring stream. After a delay of two days, in which the water dropped about three feet, another start was made only to find that the river was altogether too rough for navigation in a craft so flimsy as ours.

We consequently landed on the east bank at the mouth of a little brook with the intention of spending some days in examining the Shickshocks on the east side and getting some idea as to the probable origin of the Magdelene River. The blow-down of a few days before made travelling somewhat laborious, but one day's bushwhacking enabled us to reach a grassy plateau very similar to that which we had seen on the west side of the river. This plateau extends for many miles, is in parts rocky, with many small ponds, and apparently is an excellent feeding ground for caribou at appropriate seasons. There was much evidence that it had been used in this way in years gone by but no evidence of recent occupation, it being about as desolate a place as I have ever seen. On the south and east sides the ridge fell off very abruptly and one could see the cedar swamp of unhappy memory in

159

which we had wallowed some days before, and very clearly marked the upper portion of the Magdalene River, which here runs nearly east for a good many miles. Some of the earlier maps had indicated lakes of some proportions at the head waters of this river, but I think I am safe in saying that no lakes of any size are to be found in this area tributary to the Magdalene.

I had assumed from what the Indians had told me that at least the eastern portion of the Shickshocks would show caribou in considerable numbers. Of course I might have known that such gossip was largely or entirely without foundation, but, acting upon the assumption that it contained some modicum of truth, some three days were consumed in perambulating up and down this easterly plateau adding considerably to our experience in walking but detracting violently from the utility of our foot-wear. Tommy in particular, shod only in boot-leg oil tan moccasins, soon complained, "I walk on des damn rocks with me bare feet." Of caribou there were none, though as in the western portion there were many old horns and evidences of previous occupancy. Of wind and rain there was much, and without exaggeration it may be said that camping in a rain storm on this bleak, wind-blown plateau where anchorage for a tent was of the slimmest and wood scarce, dry, and tough, added notably to our ability to be happy though cold.

At the end of this time we judged that the St. Anne River would perhaps have returned to something like its normal water level and might therefore be navigable in the little canoe. Tommy was avidly interested in the position of the falls and kept inquiring, "Where you suppose dose falls?" Since his information was quite the equal of mine which was absolutely nil, our general progress down the practically continuous rapids of the river was not without interest. An amusing and for the moment stimulating incident occurred at the very start. We found that the water had subsided considerably, but immediately below where we had left our canoe was a long rocky rapid, quite obviously no place to run on a paddle. In loading the canoe I observed that Tommy placed both paddles on the bottom and proceeded nicely to adjust his load amidships where there was no cross-thwart. I remonstrated, pointing out to him that I was not myself a past master with a pole and that I felt safer with a paddle on the top of the load. He replied quite properly, "Dat no place for paddle. Got to drop with pole." However, we compromised by tucking the paddle under the forward thwart so that its handle lay convenient to my hand. In this rather rough and perfectly unknown water Tommy ran bow, it being my business simply to retard progress and keep us straight with the current.

We had not gone a hundred yards before Tommy's pole became jammed between two rocks in such a way that he must either abandon it, break it, or upset the canoe. He took the wise alternative of letting it go. At precisely the same moment my pole broke just at the level of my upper hand leaving me with about five feet of the stump, and Tommy with none. Without a word he reached for my paddle and we finished the balance of a half mile rapids on the principle of avoiding the rocks and trusting to the Lord. In the pool at the bottom Tommy remarked grinningly, "Dat good little paddle. We best go shore cut new poles."

From this point to the falls was a succession of moderate rapids with intervening quiet stretches which occupied about three days and I suppose was not over fifty miles since we proceeded cautiously, always dropping through rapids on a pole because of our complete ignorance of the position of the falls. These proved as usual to be much less formidable than stated. They were in fact three pitches too rough to run, aggregating perhaps fifty feet and ending in a beautiful pool, literally swarming with salmon. Hunger is an imperious mistress. Though entirely prepared to plead guilty to the charge of unsportsmanlike conduct, it must be admitted that a handsome salmon fell victim to a wooden spear. We had no tackle and nothing from which a spear could be constructed. The salmon were numerous. Tommy alleged that he could spear one with a contrivance which he could make with an axe and crooked knife. The salmon were duly speared.

Some twenty miles of practically dead water brought us on a Sunday morning to St. Anne des Monts, a little fishing village at the mouth of the river apparently at the moment wholly void of inhabitants. It developed, however, that they were concealed in the church, but I was little better off when they appeared since their language, which I had supposed was a French patois, was quite beyond me, and my alleged French quite beyond them. Tommy refused to talk though I have always suspected that he knew the language and could speak it fluently. After some hours of communication chiefly by signs it appeared that the only method of returning to the neighborhood of civilization was by a steamer which ran from Gaspé Basin to Quebec twice a week. It was alleged to arrive at St. Anne des Monts between ten and eleven o'clock at night and would stop for passengers. On the night of the third day, in inky darkness, it arrived about two miles off shore. There was a moderate swell running in the Gulf and the negotiation of the distance at night in the cockle shell was at all times interesting. The water was full of phosphorus and each wave and paddle stroke was marked with silver.

In the gray dawn of the following morning we disembarked in the cockle shell about two miles off Father Point in a not inconsiderable sea-way having been advised by the captain that we should certainly drown. As the water was cold and the hour early we carefully avoided following his prediction and routed out the sleepy keeper of the light house in search of breakfast. From here we could return to Campbellton by train and the circuit was thus complete.

As the result of this ramble I was well-satisfied that the St. Anne and the Little Cascapedia have in the past constituted a thoroughly satisfactory portage route from the Gulf of the St. Lawrence to the Bay of Chaleur. At any reasonable pitch of water the St. Anne would have been readily navigable with only two short portages, one at the Falls and one at St. Anne Lake. If, as may be assumed, the route was used with reasonable frequency, the Little Cascapedia would have been kept sufficiently free from log jams to be a thoroughly navigable stream. I do not doubt that this was a route more or less regularly employed by the Indians and giving them ready access to New Brunswick, Maine, and if they desired, to Massachusetts Bay.

Photo by Benjamin Chew.

ON A MORAIN ABOVE KOK-SU

CHAPTER VII.

Ibex and Poli in High Thian-Shan

By Benjamin Chew

In 1909 Harrison and I decided to go to Thian-Shan and try for the great *Ibex siberica* and *Ovis poli* — and what a trip it was!

I kept a very careful journal of it and it is from this that I am going to translate direct and with no alteration, the account of the killing of my big ram and of the day of days, when the great herd of buck ibex charged all about me in the high pinnacles of those mighty mountains, and of how I took toll of them.

Of Sultan Bek and Kudai Kildi, our faithful shikaris, of Barth, our traitorous interpreter, of all the adventures and vicissitudes of that long journey — I have not, in this chapter, the space to expand. Suffice it to say that it was a grand and glorious trip, and that even after all these years the events which took place stand out clear and bright in my memory.

I begin quoting from my entries in the journal on August 9, 1909:

Monday, August 9th. Camp on the Kin-Su. We

decided, last night, to move camp across the Kok-Su, as the water had fallen enough for us to ford it, and to move up to fresh grounds on the Kin-Su, a tributary. I started from camp at 6:30, with Sultan and a Kazak with my lunch, to make a day of it on the way to the new camp. We went up a small stream that runs into the Kok-Su, just North of the Kin-Su, and saw George and his men going up the right-hand mountain just ahead of us, he having started some fifteen minutes earlier. So we went up the left-hand mountain, and as we neared the top of the first ridge, we saw at the summit a herd of Teke (Ibex) and my hopes rose, only however to be dashed when, on looking through the glasses, we found them to be young ones and nannies. I was much disappointed, but started to spy the surrounding country for possible bucks, when Sultan, who had the glasses at the time, pointed across the canon to a draw low down on the right-hand mountain and said, "Kulja!" (rams). I looked and saw against the grass, what in my enthusiasm of three weeks ago I should have immediately pronounced sheep, but with the wisdom of my many disappointments, I said, "Yook, yook; tash!" ("No, no; stones!") at which Sultan laughed and handed me the glasses, and sure enough, on looking, I found a bunch of eight or ten big and little rams. It is needless to say that I was overjoyed, and that ibex went

166

out of my head instanter. After looking for George, to make sure that he was not after them, and seeing him disappearing over the ridge a mile or more away, we hurried down the mountain we had just climbed, and making a long detour, to avoid any possibility of the rams getting our wind, which at that time of day (9:15 A.M.) was blowing up the draw (canon), we came to the ridges above and behind the rams. There we left our horses, and made the last part of the climb on foot, reaching a cliff about 175 yards above the rams,— just one hour after we had first seen them. Cautiously peering over the grassy brink, we saw them still lying where we had seen them, and I proceeded to pick the best head;— not an easy thing to do, as they were all lying down, and the weather being very hazy, one could not see too well. I consulted with Sultan Bek, and by means of arranging pebbles in the respective positions in which the rams lay, I found that he considered the biggest the same one that I did, so I took up my position for a shot; but found it rather far and very awkward. Not wishing to risk a miss, I decided to climb down the ridge another hundred yards. This we did — with great difficulty — and I reached a fair place to shoot from. On my looking over, one of those beastly little ground-hackeys, or hedge-hogs, started whistling at me, and disturbed the rams, so that I had to make up my mind quickly, as one or two of the smaller rams got on their feet and looked in my direction, though I doubt if they saw me. At any rate, I took careful aim at my big fellow, who was lying with his back toward me, and drawing it rather low, to allow for the trajectory, pulled the trigger. How they jumped and ran! But I had hit my sheep, and I knew that he would not go far, so I tried to get another out of the bunch as they ran, and I thought I did hit one, as he disappeared over the ridge.

Sultan signalled to the Kazak to bring up the horses, while I dashed down the cliff as fast as I could, falling all over myself, but getting down safely to where they had lain, and there, sure enough, where the big one had been, was thick clotted blood, showing he had been hit.

The horses soon came up, and we went up the ridge after the sheep, sending the Kazak around the base, to look for a second ram. We no sooner topped that ridge than on the one beyond, we saw two rams standing, about 400 yards away, and I was about to shoot when they started running,— having seen the Kazak below. I shelled them, but did not hit them, the bullets falling short, but I thought that they must be the wounded ones, and was cursing that Kazak for showing himself, when out from under my feet, almost from under the ridge on which I was standing, bolted my big fellow.

THE GREATEST OF ALL WILD SHEEP — OVIS POLI

I was surprised, and almost forgot to shoot, but recovered in time to give him two barrels — right and left — both of which struck him, and down he went, to my intense satisfaction, as I now saw that he was a very fine large specimen. Just as we got to him, he started to roll down the steep mountain side, and would have gone 1000 feet or more had I not jumped from my pony and made a grab for his hind leg, which whirled by me at that moment, and dragged me with it. I hung on and stopped him.

He measured 54 inches around the curve, 18 inches around the butt, and 41 inches, tip to tip. So I have a corking good head! We skinned him and sent the Kazak home with him, and then we started up the mountain after the other two; but though we found their track, there was no blood, so I don't think I hit them.

We worked on till we reached the tops, however, and there found G's track, and saw the body of a fine Teke he had shot. Seeing nothing more we started for camp, and it was lucky we did, for with tired horses, the way was long and very bad. We got in at seven o'clock.

Tuesday, August 24th. Camp on a Small Stream between the Kuk-Terek and Kuk-Su. Later, found out that it was called Cholok-Terek.

We awoke, today, to a sky of cloud-rack and mists,

and the promise of the morning was well fulfilled during the day, as it rained on and off all the time, and now, at six o'clock, is pouring.

Two of the cook's boxes are lost somewhere on the mountain and consequently we are starving. Two of the Kazaks are sick, one spitting blood and coughing horribly, and the other holding his middle and moaning like a lost soul. We gave the first 15 grs. of quinine, and the second, some brandy, hot water and Jamaica ginger, followed by the application of two of my mustard plasters, — which are hot enough, as I know from experience.

We should make the Kok-Su and shooting grounds in another day, if all goes well.

Wednesday, August 25th. Camp on another stream between Kuk-Terek and Kuk-Su. We came over the roughest trail we have so far encountered, and the horses, which were in bad enough shape to begin with, were all done up by yesterday's hard march, especially the two which played out on the mountain, and did not get in until late. We crossed the mountains by a pass which under more favorable circumstances would not have seemed so steep, but it was all the tired horses could do to get up it. We dropped down into the next valley and there made camp, just in time to avoid the rain, which having threatened all morning, came down in a pour, about four o'clock.

Thursday, August 26th. Same Camp. We spent the day procuring new horses and making our arrangements for our departure from this camp, which we are going to leave under the care of Puss in Boots. Tomorrow we are going to cross a mountain over which only one Kirghiz has been and into a new and practically unknown country, where no white men have been and only one or two Kirghiz hunters, as the flocks are never taken in there. Consequently, we travel very light, with only the small tent and shelter tent, our beds and enough food for a week. We have to start at daylight tomorrow, to cross the snow-fields, before the frost of the night softens, so that our horses can travel on top. From here, the mountains look formidable and I don't know what the day may bring forth.

It has been cloudy, rainy and cold all today, and this makes the fifth bad day we have had in succession. As there were indications of a sunset and the clouds seemed to thin out this evening, it may be clear tomorrow. I sincerely hope so.

The people from whom we got the horses, today, are Kara Kirghiz, — the tribe to which belong Kudi Kildi and Sultan Bek.

George expects to go one way and I the other, when we get over the mountains, and we will probably not see one another again till we get back to this camp.

Friday, August 27th. Camp on a small stream in deep gorge, S.E. of Kok-Su.

We departed from camp, this morning, at six o'clock, leaving Barth in charge of the two big tents, provisions, .303 rifles and shot-gun, and in fact, all the impedimenta except the two small tents and enough food to last us for a week. We are compelled to travel very light, owing to the steepness and roughness of the trail, — as a matter of fact, there is no trail. From camp we went up, up, up — a long narrow valley, down the middle of which boiled a glacial torrent; the steep sides up which the so-called trail led being boggy, when not a mass of broken rock.

Rounding a bend in the valley, we came in sight of a tremendous glacier, entirely filling the far end, like a great white marble amphitheatre, rising at first in great rolling masses, and then more and more steeply, until it formed a vast semi-circular scarp of glittering ice and snow against the azure of the early morning sky. How we were ever to get over it was a question George and I asked ourselves, and we speculated on which point we were to scale that seemingly unsurmountable barrier. Our Kirghiz guide seemed, however, little daunted by it, and over it he led us, up and up, across crevasses and fissures that made our blood run cold to look down into, and into one of which a pack horse actually did fall part way, and was drawn out with difficulty. Up and up, until the air was so thin and cold that one's lungs seemed about to burst, and one's heart pounded like the throb of a high-speed motor, till at last, floundering through snow up to the horses' bellies, we reached the crest of the scarp, and gazed out over a view of the great peaks of Thian-Shan, which near and far raised their rocky cliffs and snow-capped tops high out of the misty blue of those deep and precipitous gorges, the like of which exist nowhere else in the world.

We now had to go down a slope as steep as that which we had just come up, and far worse for the horses, as it was all slide rock, and cut their feet cruelly. Down, down, we dropped, as we had come up, — slowly and painfully, — till at last we came again to the grass slopes, and these, bad as they were, now seemed paradise indeed, after the awful going we had just passed over.

At this point, I, — who with G., was bringing up the rear, — was considerably startled by a loud report, as of a gigantic blast, and looking up, saw, just about where I thought our leading men should be, a great mass of rock separate itself, in a cloud of dust, from the face of the beetling cliffs which overhung the valley, and dash down with a thundering roar into the torrent, hundreds of feet below.

Luckily, it was farther on than I thought and none

of our people were near it; but it gave me a very unpleasant feeling, while passing beneath those frowning rocks that lined our way.

About 12:30 it became cloudy, and great masses of vapour swirled about the peaks and at times filled the valleys, so that twice we had to stop and await its clearing. It was during one of these intermittent spells, when the clouds for a moment allowed us to see the tops of the ridges, that Sultan Bek espied on the skyline a herd of Ibex, which on examination through the glasses, proved to be a large herd of bucks. The caravan was immediately stopped, and after an argument with George, in which I begged him to accompany me, which he, with his usual generosity refused to do, saying that he wished me to get a good head, and that two shooting would be apt to spoil my chance, — I set out at a little after one o'clock, with Sultan Bek and a Kazak, to hold the horses.

We were able to ride only a short distance up the slopes, owing to their extreme steepness; indeed, they seemed little out of the perpendicular, and at one-thirty, we left the horses and took to our legs.

I had an awful time, as the grass was soaking wet and I had on my field boots, out of which all the hob nails had long since departed, so that it was with the greatest difficulty that I was able to keep a foot-hold.

The rocks were almost as bad as the grass, as the wet leather slipped on them badly.

We climbed steadily for an hour, the clouds getting thicker and thicker about us, until on the brink of an almost unseen chasm, we had to stop and wait. It then started to hail and rain, and the wind cut like a razor; but at last it cleared up a bit, enough for us to see a few hundred yards about us, and up again we started, higher and higher, until when nearing the top of the ridge, we saw on the grass slope, just under the topmost cliffs, the Ibex!

There must have been some seventy bucks, all told; big and little, and a wonderful sight they were. I was puffing so, and my heart was playing such a tattoo on my ribs, after the hard climb, that I could hardly hold the glasses steady enough to see through.

The Ibex were some 350 yards away, and it was very hard to make out the big ones at such a distance and in the bad light, so with the utmost caution and very painfully, we crawled along the face of the mountain, taking advantage of every bit of cover — which, however, was scant — and at last got to a good position about 200 yards away from them, on a projecting buttress of rock, on which I got a very precarious foot-hold, and from which I tried to pick the biggest buck. A hard job, however, as the fog was very bad and there were many fine heads.

Suddenly something frightened them, luckily on the side away from me, and they all jumped to their feet and bunched together, so that I saw many which until then had been feeding or lying down, out of my range of vision, and had a better chance to choose a good head. They made for the crest of the ridge at once, but luckily for me, stopped before reaching it. I had by then picked a good head and at last made up my mind to fire, though the light and distance made it chancy. I did so, and wounded my big fellow. Now there came to me that luck of which every sports-man dreams,* of which we sometimes read, and which occurs but once in a thousand times, and then, alas! to some poor chap who probably only has two shells, or is too puffed to shoot, or has some other reason why he cannot take advantage of it.

But this was the thousand and first time, and I was, thank the Lord, able to take advantage of it, though

* NOTE: George Harrison watched the entire proceedings from the camp which he had made in the Nullah, almost directly below the peaks where all this was taking place. He told me afterwards, that his idea of why the Ibex charged towards me at the first report of my rifle was that a small cloud of vapor had, some minutes before I fired, enveloped Sultan Bek and myself, and had then floated down into the Nullah away from the Ibex. It had then met an up current of air which had drifted it upward and over the Ibex, and undoubtedly bore the scent of our bodies to them, and, coming from down the Nullah, naturally had driven them toward us! This seems to be the best explanation of their action, as the wind, while not directly from us to them, was of necessity, shaved very fine by us, and was blowing down the Nullah as it always does at that time of day. The up current, due to the cloudy and unsettled con-dition of the weather, undoubtedly served us well!

Photo courtesy of Field Museum of Natural History.

HIGH ON THE CLIFF WE SAW A MAGNIFICENT HEAD

probably not so well as a really good shot would have done. At all events, it was one of the greatest and most exciting moments of my life. The Ibex for some reason or other — probably because they had already been startled from the other side — no sooner heard the report of my first shot, than they dashed directly toward me, and in a moment I was surrounded by Ibex — above me, below me, all about me!

Of course I was wild with excitement, as was Sultan Bek, who kept shouting, "Tekke chong! Tekke chong!" pointing every which way, — which did not aid me in the hard job of selecting the big heads as they appeared and disappeared, all too quickly, among the rocks. However, I tried to keep my head and managed to shoot six of the biggest. Three dropped dead near me, and I was able to get in several more shots at wounded ones, as they went down the precipitous cliffs on the other side of the mountain. The fog had closed in again so thickly that I was only able to see a very short distance, and so it was chance shooting, and I shall have to trust to to-morrow to getting my wounded ones.

It was 4:30 when I started shooting, so George tells me, who saw the whole thing through his glass, from thousands of feet below. Sultan Bek and I skinned out the heads and cut them off the bodies, which we rolled down the mountain to where we were going to camp, and then Sultan shouldered two of the heads and I the other and my rifles and glasses, and started down the mountain. About half way down, we met one of the Kazaks, whom George had sent up. He was bare-footed! I suppose that he could not keep a footing in the wet and slippery grass in his high heeled riding boots. Despite that, he shouldered the two heads that Sultan was carrying, and I gladly relinquished him mine, and went on with only my rifle, which, however, got heavier and heavier. I don't know how many times I fell. It got quite dark and the rain started to pour, and to make matters worse, I came across innumerable badger holes in the long grass, into which I plunged, every few steps. Once I stepped out into space and thought I was gone, but found myself, a second later, sprawling in a soft bed of wet weeds. Despite all these vicissitudes, I reached camp at last at 7:30, with every muscle aching, but in the highest good humor and monstrously elated by my greatest day's shooting.

Saturday, August 28th. Same Camp. I slept the sleep of the weary, which is not always the soundest and best. In fact I was so tired that I did not sleep at all well until morning, when just about the time I had to get up, I fell into that delightful deep sleep, which only the business man and commuter knows; out of which I was awakened about seven by

Sultan Bek, who was, I think, as tired as myself.

I said good-bye to George, who is off down the valley into the pines after maral (Wapiti) and whom I do not expect to see again until we both get back to the main camp.

We started out at eight, on horseback, and managed to reach the ridges mounted, though it was a frightful climb, and we went up places where I had never thought a horse could go. We left the tired beasts on the ridge in charge of the Kazak, and started down the cliffs on the other side, and after about half an hour's rough going, came across one of the wounded Ibex. I put another shot into him, but it was a snap shot and I hit him high up and rather far back and away he went. I saw that he had a very bad wound in his near thigh, and the blood trail that he left was enough to lead a blind man. He led us a merry dance, however, up and down the most impossible places, for nearly an hour and a half; but at last we caught him, resting back of a pinnacle, and after some maneuvering, I got into a place where I could get a shot at him. Not, however, before he jumped up and was starting off again. I caught him, though, this time, — right through the heart, and he turned a double somersault and went plunging over and over, hundreds of feet down the cliffs; bumping here and there, and sometimes hitting on his horns, when he would give an extra high bound. I was afraid there would be nothing left when we got to him, but luckily, no great damage was done. One of his horns was broken off mid-way, but that had been done long ago, — how I have no idea. The other, however, makes up for it by being huge. It measures fifty-four inches!

We got back to the horses at 1:30 and had some lunch, and then started off on the trail of another of the wounded Ibex, and after about an hour's climbing, came upon him, lying at the foot of a slide, with his head turned under him, his horns buried deep in the stony soil, quite dead. He proved to be a very fine head, too, and thank Heaven, his horns were not broken. They measured forty-seven inches.

After skinning him out, a job not easy on an incline of 45 degrees, we got back to the horses and to camp, which I was thankful to reach.

Sunday, August 29th. Same Camp. Two days' hard work left me pretty well played out, this morning, especially as I have slept badly for these last two nights. But the idea of the game on the mountain above me has acted as enough of a stimulant to keep me going, and so I was off again, this morning, at eight, and reached the top on horseback, after an hour and a half. We again left the horses in the same place and struck out on the trail of the herd, which though faint, after the rain yesterday and the day before, was still visible.

At about eleven o'clock we were rewarded by seeing the bucks at the base of some cliffs on the far side of a circular rock slide, some 500 yards off, as the crow flies. It was farther than that to get to them, however, as we had to climb down the ridge on which we were perched and get over the rock slide, — no easy job.

The wind was wrong, too, and they must have gotten a puff of it, for they moved off, though slowly, and disappeared.

We were resting for a moment to get our wind and I was trying to spy the bucks through my glasses, when suddenly I caught sight of a single Ibex, high up among the cliffs below which I had first seen the herd. A glance sufficed to show me that he was a very big head, and a second, that he was wounded. I knew that I had at last found the big fellow, the king of the herd, I believed, which I had wounded and lost in the fog on Friday. He had seen us, unfortunately, before we saw him, and though he had an awful wound in the stern, and another .450 bullet in his abdomen, as I afterwards found out, he went up those cliffs in a remarkable manner and led us a long chase up most stupendous pieces of rock, almost to the top of the mountain, whither Sultan Bek and I pursued him, with vast exertion at the imminent risk of our necks.

We passed through what I think must be the Ibex paradise; ledges covered with moss, no wider than a man's hand; shelves in the cliffs where a little green grass grew — how I don't know — but where an Ibex could curl up and lie down, and have a nibble; little rills of sparkling water, new from the snow, not far above, which danced down polished runnels in the yellowish rock; shade and sunlight, and above all, almost absolute security from bears, wolves, and — I was going to say — from man.

But somehow or other, we managed to worm our way along these narrow ledges, and at last came upon our quarry, some 40 yards above us. I finished him with a shot back of the shoulder, just as he was making one more frantic effort to get away. He came down the rocks, head over heels, almost on top of us, and Sultan just saved his going over a cliff with a drop of 100 feet or more, by pluckily catching his hind leg as he whirled by, and by still more pluckily holding on, to the very brink of the chasm.

We had quite a time skinning him, and a good deal of excitement getting him down the cliffs. The strap from my rifle was very useful, and with it we handed him down from one to the other, from ledge to ledge, until we were once more safely down on the rock slide, — which now, by comparison, seemed easy and tame; though two months ago, it would have taken all my nerve to cross it.

The head was a really magnificent one, — by far the finest I have ever seen. It measured fifty-two inches around the curve, and spread *forty-six inches, tip to tip!*

We got back to the horses at half past three, and back to camp a little more than an hour later. It had been a glorious day, — the first for many. The air was clear and sparkling, a delight to breathe, and I got a most wonderful view of the whole Thian-Shan range, stretching away for miles — till their rocks and snows were lost in the purple haze of infinite distance.

CHAPTER VIII.

Gemsbuck on the Molopo

By George L. Harrison

In June of 1913 my wagon was standing on the Molopo River in the Kalahari Desert where I had gone to get a couple of good gemsbuck heads.

In addition to the usual complement of servants, I had two Bushmen and an after rider of mixed blood who took care of the horses.

The Molopo was now a river only in name, for although the rains were just over there was no running water, only fast drying pools several miles apart.

I was on the edge of the Gemsbuck country, a region better known to sportsmen in the last century than in this. Since the opening up of British East Africa, South Africa has been forgotten. A mile or so on each side of where I was camped was a brak or salt lick to which gemsbuck, wildebeest and Cape Hartebeeste came on several nights in the week, but always left long before dawn to travel back many miles to their own country. As one left the river there was first a belt of large timber a mile or more across — then two or three miles of high thorn bush. After this came ten miles of grassy plain interspersed with clumps of lower thorn. Beyond this was the sand dune country the gemsbuck seemed to like so well.

Often I would take up the spoor of a gemsbuck at the brak at dawn and follow it in a direct line back from the river until it was so late in the day that I had to return to camp. These animals, I think, must have traveled great distances from the interior to get salt.

Occasionally an animal would only travel a few miles into the open plain before stopping to rest or feed. If it were resting it would usually make a loop and lie down where it could see its back track as moose are so apt to do, or if feeding would take numerous tacks down wind, often stopping to watch its back track. Incessantly hunted with poisoned arrows by the Bushmen, the game was exceedingly wary. I wasted a week trying to get a shot in this way and at last gave it up, as I always met with failure. I decided that the gemsbuck might be more difficult to approach near the river than they would be in the dunes which was their own country. On several occasions when we followed the spoor directly back from the river and into the dunes, I had seen a great deal of spoor, both old and new. Also the rolling dunes would make approach easier.

If I had known, before leaving Mafeking, what the country was like, I would have taken a number of empty barrels, filled half of them at a pool and trekked back twenty miles from the river. Making camp I would have sent the wagon back to the river to bring the other barrels when needed. As it was very cold — some of the pools in the shade were frozen over all day — we would not have needed much water for the horses or men. I would have been saved a long ride every day and my Bushmen a long trot in front of my pony. I only once came up with gemsbuck before they reached the dunes and on that occasion had a remarkable experience.

My men had that morning picked up the spoor of four gemsbuck at the brak and had followed it, at a trot, until the animals had begun to feed —not true grazing, but taking a bite here and there as they went along. At last I saw them in front and rather spread out as they stopped occasionally to crop a favorite herb. I pushed on after them, but whether by luck or design one had remained behind in some thorns and at once gave the alarm before I was within shot. Stepping into the open, I took out my field glasses to watch them disappear in the distance, and before taking them from my eyes swept the country to my left. At what seemed through the glasses to be at my very feet, I saw a gemsbuck fast asleep. He was lying a hundred and fifty yards away, nose resting on the ground and horns straight up in the air. The sun glinting from his horns as they imperceptibly moved in his deep breathing had called my attention to him. It did not take us long to sink down and begin to crawl nearer. On account of the dry grass, here knee high, I could not see the gemsbuck, but the upper parts of his horns showed that he was still asleep. I had hoped to get a shot at fifty yards, but on account of the ground had to get nearer. This my bushman objected to vigorously, plucking at my sleeve and whispering "Shellum Bass, Shellum" (A Rogue sir — a Rogue).

Leaving him behind, I went on until I was within twenty yards of the sleeping bull. Getting into a sitting position I cocked my rifle and sat quietly until I got my wind. A low whistle brought the bull to his feet facing me and with the foresight on his broad chest I pulled the trigger of the right barrel. A click was the only result. Thinking I had forgotten to load, I quietly opened the barrels to find that it had been a miss fire. By the time I closed the rifle the bull had ducked around a patch of thorn and I never saw him again. The above experience seems to contradict my account of the great wariness of the gemsbuck, but perhaps it is the exception which proves the rule.

As I had been working hard from dawn until dark for a week without success, I decided before taking a rest to go the next day directly to the dune country where I had the good fortune to kill a gemsbuck bull with horns 40½ inches in length. I had been told that anything over 35 inches was very good and felt that now my trip was a success. We brought the head in that night and sent the wagon driver and voor looper the next day with four yoke of oxen to bring in the beast. Taking the horse's back spoor they easily found the place. Cutting down a thorn tree, they put the gemsbuck on this improvised sled and dragged it in.

After a day of well earned rest, I was off the second morning direct to the dunes and found plenty of spoor but saw no game. About three o'clock we came on some fresh tracks and were following them along a wide shallow valley some miles in length, when suddenly my Bushman stopped and told me that a gemsbuck bull had just crossed the valley and was feeding over the sand dunes on the right. All tracks in the sand looked like marks made by a walking stick in the dry sand of the seaside, but I knew my men could read them like a book, so over the dune I went and got a good bull.

We were many miles from camp but a full moon rose at sundown and by its light we rode a great part of the way. As we were riding along in the cold, our tired horses suddenly whirled around and galloped off in a panic caused by our having reached the track made in bringing in the other gemsbuck two days before. A good example of the excellent noses possessed by horses which are not stabled.

Although countless thousands of game animals had used the braks for centuries there were no game paths leading to them nor are there any game paths in this part of Africa. In fact with the exception of Elephant roads, I have never seen game paths in Africa such as we find in America. The desiccation of South Africa is held by some authorities to be largely due to the introduction of domestic animals which make paths to and from the "fountains" or springs, thus turning what would otherwise be marshes to deep gulleys and causing great erosion of the soil.

Whatever the cause, this part of Africa is fast drying up. In 1836 Cornwallis Harris' camp on the Molopo was invaded by a hippo. Now the river, 150 to 200 yards in width, is dry for the greater part of the year.

Around one of the braks the Bush people had built a fence of thorn bushes with game pits at intervals inside. The greater part of this fence had been destroyed by fire but there was still a small section left with the pits still covered. The hedge where the pits were was lower than the rest, being about two feet high, so that an animal would jump this part and land on the covering of the pit. The pits were four feet deep and sunk in the bottom of each was a gems-

buck skull with horns attached. The skull was imbedded in the clay of the pit bottom — a very deadly
weapon. One day in passing the brak which had the
remains of the thorn hedge, we found that a large
gemsbuck cow, in her eagerness to join others in the
brak, had jumped the fence and landed in a pit. The
horns, sunk in the bottom of the pit, had pierced her
through and through and showed above her withers.
Death must have come quickly. Gemsbuck, like other
desert loving animals, can live for long periods without water and I was surprised to find that of the
many gemsbuck which used the braks none ever went
to drink at the pools which lay within a few yards of
each brak. In Kordofan I was once camped sixty miles
from a deep well and this well was the only known
water for miles around. In spite of this the country
was full of game. In both instances the grass and
foliage were very dry. The few patches of wild mel-
ons could not have gone far in supplying moisture.

Of all the men I have ever had, Pony and Tacker,
my Bushmen, were by far the best spoorers. When it
is realized that the country was a sandy desert in
which the spoor of animals looked like holes poked in
the sand with a walking stick, their skill can be appreciated. They could tell within an hour or so how old
the spoor was and could read the signs like a book.
Both had the stamina usually associated with their

race and for days at a time could trot for miles in front of the horses. This was all the more remarkable as they both smoked hemp all night and their shrieks when in the delirium, which follows a few puffs of the pipe, would drown the chorus of the Jackals. They had on their bellies and thighs the grayish scars caused by burns received from sleeping too near a fire on cold nights and which earned their kind the name of "Witspens" bestowed by the Boers.

Sir Francis Galton records that two women with their feet cut off came into his camp. In a raid these women had been surprised by another tribe, who cut off their feet as the easiest way of getting their anklets. The women poked the stumps in the sand to stop the bleeding and then lived on roots and berries until they found him. When Pony and Tacker found a bee tree they would put their arms in the hole and get out the honey regardless of the numerous stings they received.

After getting my two gemsbuck and the one in the game pit, I turned my attention to Cape hartebeeste and wildebeest, getting good specimens of each variety. There were also kudu near the river, but as I had shot these before I did not look for them.

This part of Africa is a delightful country with enough game to suit anyone not out to kill. The days are brilliant and the nights very cold. Sand grouse, guinea fowl and ducks add variety to the pot.

From my Journal: September 9th, 1908.

The Kafue River joins the Zambesi from the North and when in spate overflows parts of the adjoining country with the result that all burrowing animals are drowned, and when the flood subsides a luxuriant crop of grass comes up. This grass grows to the height of eight or ten feet, and under months of a cloudless sky becomes in time as dry as tinder. It is then burned by the natives leaving a bed of ashes through which new shoots of grass spring from the old roots.

Attracted by the new grass as well as by the river, in what at this season is becoming a rapidly drying country, wildebeest, hartebeeste, roan antelope and zebra come in thousands to join the great herds of letchwe already there. The particular part of the country where we reached the river is called the Kafue Flats, and I am told that they are fifty miles long by about twenty broad. Whether this is true or not, I do not know, but I do know that to the West of our camp the land is level as the sea and as featureless as far as the eye could reach.

We reached the Flats late last night — as here we could follow the good maxim that the sun should never, if possible, shine on oxen in the yoke — and had camped under a single tall palm, the only tree in sight. This palm grew on the flat top of a low ridge about twenty feet above the plain, thus giving a better view than otherwise could be obtained and serving besides as a better landmark.

This morning I had finished breakfast before the dawn and was impatiently awaiting the coming day to see the Flats about which I had heard so much. The first rays of the sun rising behind us shone on a wonderful sight, for as far as the glass could reach were to be seen herds of game numbering many thousands showing plainly in the clear morning air.

In my other trips to Africa I have done all my shooting on foot, but here was a chance to use my shooting ponies in the old South African fashion of galloping up to the game and shooting from the saddle. I have two ponies, one very handy and very slow, the other very fast but needing a square mile to turn in when extended. Ten days ago I killed an Eland on the fast one at the risk of my life, as I very narrowly escaped being brained by low limbs and falling into burrows of all kinds. Here was a country without a tree or burrow, thanks to the floods, and level as a Polo field, with as sound going.

A few minutes after dawn found me cantering from camp accompanied by Finaughty to help with any game I might shoot, who in turn was followed on foot by a crowd of meat hungry natives.

What more could one ask than to be on a good horse in the cool of a beautiful morning as he cantered along with arched neck playing with the bits of the double bridle.

Half a mile away a large herd of wildebeest was moving off at my approach with the usual bucks and kicks which, if drawn by an artist, would be thought to be greatly exaggerated. These before long settled down to a fast gallop as I increased my pace and soon joined a herd of roan antelope adding to the cloud of dust and ashes which the wildebeest were kicking up.

I was now galloping as fast as I could, but as herd after herd of game joined in, the clouds of ashes and dust were so dense that I could see nothing but the tails of a great band of zebras bringing up the rear — a few strides more put me among these as the pace was too fast for them and I nearly came to grief through taking my foot from the stirrup and kicking a fat old stallion in the ribs as he wallowed along beside me, mouth open, gasping for breath. He was so near that the jar of my kick made my pony cross his legs and for some yards he traveled on nose as well as knees, while I narrowly escaped going over his head. By the time I had regained the lost ground more herds had joined in and the clouds of dust and ashes were so thick that I could not see a length ahead, nor could I see the sun. There was nothing to do but pull up and wait until the slight breeze which had come up with the dawn had blown the clouds away.

In time Finaughty found me and we cantered along until we came to a great herd of letchwe. These antelope have a habit in common with certain other animals in Asia and Africa of crossing the bows of anyone riding toward them, so one could always get a shot by riding in a parallel course when they would cross in front giving time to jump off and select a good head. This expedient I tried and while waiting for a good head to pass, I saw from the tail of my eye a herd of zebras crossing behind me. When I could look around I found that my pony had joined them, galloping with his head on one side so as not to step on the reins, a trick that showed he was an old hand at this game, although until now he had been as steady as a rock. The gallop after game and his cousins, the zebras, had proved too much for his nerves.

Sending my after-rider to catch my horse, I set to work taking off the head of the letchwe I had shot — a task occupying a few minutes. On looking up, I saw my pony galloping away closely followed by Finaughty and they were soon out of sight. In half an hour I saw them coming towards me. They looked so near that I ran a few yards to intercept them, when to my great surprise both horses left the ground and continued galloping higher and higher in the air without apparently getting any nearer. Even then it took a few seconds for me to realize that I was seeing a wonderful mirage, very different from the stock variety of beautiful lakes and trees I had so often seen. For half an hour I watched the horses gallop, sometimes reaching an angle of 30 degrees. I saw Finaughty make several grabs at the bridle and at last catch my horse high in the air above the plain. I saw him get off his horse, loosen the girths and then get on mine, except that they were in the air apparently so close that he could hear me call. Then they started back in my direction with every detail showing plainly, but the longer they cantered the lower they got and the further off they seemed to me, until at last afar off and greatly distorted by the heat rays, I saw two tired horses approaching. As the ponies arrived from one direction, the boys joined me from the other. The letchwe was soon cut up and on its way to camp. The heat had taken the place of the cool of the morning, the horses were done, so we made for camp, letting the ponies go their own way.

After an hour's ride the palm tree appeared far off, directly between my pony' ears and no matter which direction I turned him he always swung back true as the compass when given his head. This was a very remarkable demonstration of the homing instinct, as we had only arrived at the palm tree a few hours previously and the horse had been shipped in for my use from Cape Colony, a thousand miles to the south.

CHAPTER IX.

Volcano Sheep

By G. D. POPE

It is on the broad adobe plains lying north of El Paso and hemmed to the south by the distant purple ranges that we first received the peculiar impression of the so-called "desert" or "arid" lands of the South-west. Here a large variety of the yucca plant appears, lifting on its rough, gray trunk of withered leaf-forms, its shaggy head of green and yellow, in grotesque likeness of the Indian in his war bonnet. These six-foot plants, spaced at wide intervals and running in great numbers off across the desert, appeared to bid us austere welcome to this land of little rain and drenching sunlight.

Turning west from El Paso, we traveled along the muddy banks of the Rio Grande, made green by the willows and cotton-woods of early spring, through the foothills along the border and across the dry plains. Moving ever westward we noted the changing types of vegetation, passing as it were through a panorama of this desert growth until, the quick southern night descending, we rolled into Gila Bend, disembarked bag and baggage from the Pullman and breathed with grateful lungs the sweet, fresh desert air, which seems so free from all pollution and charged with abundant energy by the long daylight of the southern sun.

The mackinaws which we had carried from the north were not uncomfortable in the chill of the March night in Arizona, at the elevation of 1,000 feet, and I recalled on the previous year the intense cold of the journey down to Ajo in the open though curtained "speeder," a gas car omnibus, which takes us to this outpost of civilization. Then, as now, the stars hung jewel bright in the great black vault, as mile after mile the little car ran smoothly over the clicking rails and we, looking out from its dark interior into the night, illuminated far ahead by the searchlight upon the roof, watched with unwearied eyes the novel, half revealed, mysterious landscape about us.

Jack rabbits hopped into the zone of our spotlight, turned a twitching ear to catch the sound of our approach and then with a leap vanished into the night. Little desert owls flew up from under the culverts, perched upon the bridge timbers for a moment, their eyes shining like green lamps, and flitted into the darkness. Once, a wildcat slinking low, ran across our path, paused a moment, with its shining eyes turned upon us, then with a bound was gone.

The steady cadence of the motor lulled us almost

to sleep on the long straight stretches, but as we neared our destination, the little car wound in and out among foothills dimly visible and suddenly we beheld in the distance a glistening diadem of light set in the velvet dark of the plain, then the cluster broke apart and became individual lights and we knew that it was Ajo, a pretty modern town of Spanish construction done in gray concrete, with its attractive plaza and band stand from which the concerts beguile the soft, sultry summer nights.

A neat modern station received us and a friendly voice told that we were expected, then a good seven-passenger car took the three of us, with our bags and guns, over to the excellent little hotel, where in clean beds we were to enjoy the first good sleep in the land of the great quiet, far from the jarring sounds of congested city life, fanned by pleasant airs that blew soft and sweet across the moonlit desert landscape to the south.

Early in the morning, Mr. Curley, Superintendent of the New Cornelia Mine, paid us a call on horse back, to find us busily unpacking and repacking for the desert trail and it was exceedingly pleasant to have his greeting and see his ruddy face and keen blue eyes and clasp his strong hand again. It was he who had made all the arrangements for our try at Pinacate and his forethought and resource, his suggestions and kindly help, contributed much to the success of our venture in this new field.

The land is strange and invites no familiarities, but my old friend, Dr. Hornaday, when he called it "Terra Incognito," was of course aware that the very road which led us southward was traveled hundreds of years ago by the early Spanish conquistadores, penetrating northward on great adventures and held a people for whom the missions were founded from San Xavier del Bac in the east (near the present Tucson) to those in the west which sought to serve and civilize the sullen, savage Yumas. To most men it is indeed an unknown land and while it tolerates and even charms those who obey the laws of the gods which dwell in that remote place, it is fierce and inexorably cruel to those who disregard the law of its life and attempt to journey there as in softer lands.

The life of the land is water, which is far and scarce and secret, and if men do not know the water or carelessly leave it behind, they may die, and if they die, die terribly.

We intended to travel from this more western and southern base by the new desert conveyance, the motor car, just as far as this would take us, but as the latter end of the trip required pack horses, we were obliged to get them off in advance and therefore spent the morning checking our food supplies and equipment, the lists for which I had mailed some weeks earlier, stowing them in the standard packing case of the southwest — a wooden box which holds two five-gallon oil cans and which, when slung with a good rope knotted into either end, forms a splendid substitute for the old raw hide pannier or alforcas.

The packing being finished and all set with final directions given for our meeting, we stood aside as Charlie untied his white saddle horse and swung aboard, gave the order to start, and led by Loretto in his blue bib-overalls and striped white shirt, the little caravan filed down the hill, through the village of Mexican shacks, built of odds and ends of lumber and old tin oilcans, and so up the dusty road, past the Glory Hole and the last evidence of modern civilization, to begin the journey across the desert toward the Gulf of California.

We had planned to give the pack outfit a good twenty-four hours' start so did not hurry our departure. We rolled out of town on the Gulf road, wound our way through the low hills in which lie the great bodies of copper ore which make Ajo, and were at last truly "headed South."

The road having been made by wagons as they found their way through the sparsely scattered clumps of mesquite, creosote bush, ocatilla, cholla plant, and what not, crossing where it could interminable small gullies deep or shallow, is full of sudden turns and sharp bends, but on the whole is decidedly good as country roads go, and we made excellent time.

We crossed great flats whose curious, changing vegetation was of ever-recurring interest — forests of the giant tree-cactus, Sahuaro, with ribbed, green, uplifted arms like Jerusalem candlesticks, the whitish silvery clusters of the cholla or choya with its ball-like burrs of poisonous spines, ready at a touch to almost leap from the parent stem to stab and torment the luckless creature barely touching it; tall, waving clusters of green-tinted rods, the graceful Ocotillo carrying at this season the brilliant cockscomb of its flower at the end of the whiplike tips, the rusty green of the creosote which is the healing herb of the desert, having disinfectant and medicinal qualities in the expressed juice of its leafage, and a gum-like caoutchouc in its twigs.

After the flats, we passed through ranges running roughly southeast by northwest across our path, first the Growler, then the Agua Dulce.

Each time we wound our way between the hills which seemed to shrink in size as we approached them, and came out again on a new plain, like the last, and yet differing from it. And so the hours passed.

We ate a snack as we ran, washing all down with the water from our canteens, which had been filled at

Ajo, their watersoaked jackets cooling their contents as they hung from top-bows of our car, sheltered from the strong Southern sunshine.

No traveler with imagination can cross a boundary line between Nations without a thrill of anticipation, and we were now approaching that generally invisible barrier which separates two peoples of the western world, the cause of many diplomatic exchanges, the ancient sanctuary toward which many a wild rider had flogged his weary horse, the fear of death in the back of his neck and gasping hope in his dark heart — for we neared the Mexican line.

One could sense no particular change as we wound cautiously down a rock-strewn hillside, working through the last low "pass," and yet presently as we emerged from a thicket of Chaparral and crossed a dry wash, Bill halted the swaying car an instant and with a wave to the left, said "There's the line," and yet the only evidence of its presence was that curious anomaly in that uninhabited land—a six-foot splinter of board, now silver gray with exposure, thrust like a spear into the body of a great suharo.

In an instant it was behind us, and the pitching car turning quickly this way and that, like a rabbit dodging through the brush, was heading east of south and making for that great landmark of the district, Cerro Colorado.

The only folks we had seen were in the survey camp located at an old ranch in a small valley at Bates Well. The few palo verde and cottonwood trees gave the place an air of green which was grateful to the eye, but except that it had a well, a windmill and some small irrigation ditches it was a pretty dry spot in which to raise crops. It was here that the only official — an immigration officer — we saw on the trip, was located, and he came out of his shack to say that he would be glad to have us come in so that he might look at our hides, if we had any, when we came back, and wished us good luck.

The country presents a curious aspect when viewed from an elevation, for one could see a great plain stretching southward out of which rose isolated peaks or small ranges, all sharply defined in that clear air, and the curious thing about these formations of disintegrating granite is that although they may actually be only one-hundred or so feet high, many are so serrated and rough, so definite in outline that they appear to be genuine mountains of normal size. The plain itself was generally of an adobe color, dotted by the sparse bushy growth which this soil supports, although in favored locations there are forests of saguaro of considerable extent and the dry water courses were generally marked by the green lines of palo verde and mesquite which manage to find moisture, the residue of rain water lying deep beneath the surface in hidden reservoirs.

In complete isolation far out on such a dun-colored plain or llano is Cerro Colorado, the Red Hill, the best known landmark of the region, a one-time cone with the upper two-thirds removed as if by a sloping cut of a giant sword.

A dark crown above the rosy brown slopes proved to be the crater, the giant gaping wound of this little volcanic hill, and this peculiarity together with its unique terra cotta red color gives it its marked personality. Beyond this, other scattering hills or buttes rise, then the plain turns from dun to black, and there, athwart our middle horizon lies the long black slopes of old Pinacate with the twin peaks midway rising sharply in beautiful cones, from the splendid long slopes on either hand. Our speedometer showed 65 miles as we drew abreast of Cerro Colorado, and halting the car, we descended upon our stiffened legs, drew our rifles out of their dusty scabbards, and walked up the gentle slope toward the crater for a look-see.

The road from here on twisted and turned with endless chuck-holes so we had an hour's very rough going, but at length the Chaparral, mesquite and greasewood was gone and we came out upon an open plain where we could take a long look in every direction, and as there was no packtrain in sight, we proceeded to unpack our gear and then sat down to smoke and wait for it.

To the north the Agua Dulce mountains were a line of ragged blue peaks, on the east, the Sonoita and Cubabi ranges hemmed us in. To the south lay Batamonte, and below it against the sky was Cerro Blanco's pale gray shape, while on our west with outlying hills and isolated heaps of brown or russet cones lay the great black mass of Pinacate, now close at hand.

From the north, presently we descried the rising dust column which marks a caravan in that land of little rain, and in time we saw a man on horseback, and then in the stillness we caught the tinkle and rattle of their packs and the thud of the tired horses' feet. The train was at hand.

The moon had risen, pale, soft and large, as we halted in a tiny valley, rounded up our stock as night fell, threw off the packs, dumped the bedrolls on the pebble-strewn adobe, got the greasewood fire going and by its cheery flames, drank our first cup of camp coffee, and ate our first camp meal.

Before the sun cleared the low hill which was the eastern doorpost of the tiny valley in which we were camped, we were out of the bags and dressed for the day, then by a mere reversal of the unrolling and strapping process of the night, our beds were made and ready to go on the pack saddle, and we ready for breakfast.

We hit an old trail deeply marked in the soil and running directly toward the peaks, where it crossed the lava. It is a well-defined grayish mark on the deep chocolate brown of crumbled rock, for it is a track worn by countless feet through many centuries.

Along the trail, as we neared our first objective, Tsinetta Tank (so I understood it), we saw the stone circles marking the Indian camp sites, always on elevated spots, where one could see all about, or hidden amid the big boulders where they were unseen.

At one we found a grinding stone, or metate, the hand-mill in which they ground mesquite beans and other seed plants, out of which crude bread or mush was made. The first tank proved to be in low water and as it was almost inaccessibly located at the bottom of a deep gully, protected by sheer overhanging cliff-walls of blue volcanic rock, we went on, only stopping to examine it, flushing a covey of quail drinking there. The water itself, a pool perhaps fifteen feet square and ten feet deep, looked fairly clean where the green floating scum had been brushed aside with a branch, and tasted sweet and cool, shaded as it was by the high rock wall. We went a mile further up the same arroyo and found another, a double upper and lower tank, El Capitan, and it being a favorable spot, we pitched camp on the slope or ridge above it.

One usually thinks of pitching camp as the clearing of sites and erection of tents under shady trees near a pleasant stream, but this was a very different matter. There was one tree, a palo verde, perhaps ten feet high, in whose shade we hung our well-soaked canteens to cool by evaporation, and the cook, as the wooden panniers were lifted from the horses, set them 'round the spot which was to be his kitchen fireplace and cleaned the ground of brush and loose stone which might harbor snakes or bugs.

The upper tank, accessible to horses over a rather steep trail down some rock ledges, was dry, but in a nearby cave we found a kerosene tin left by some earlier party, and we soon had a bail rigged on it, and with a rope lifted water up the rock wall, from the lower pool and filled the upper, which was about the size of a horse trough. The grateful animals fairly crowded the men off the ledge in their eagerness to plunge their muzzles in the pool.

After lunch, it being too late to get in a real hunt, we scouted the nearby lava fields and explored some big gullies, but save a few quail, and the doves which were flitting incessantly all around the camp, we saw no sign of game.

The shadows lengthened as we came back into camp and the sun soon dropped behind the black shoulder of Pinacate, leaving us to finish our evening meal in the brief twilight, and make down our beds by the light of the fire and our flashlights.

Tired as we were, the moon actually kept us awake, it was so near and luminous, but after awhile the big silence weighed down our eyelids and we were in deep restful slumber.

One thing was obvious — the conditions were very unlike those in northern sheep country; the weather was warm, not cold; the hills were bare, not timbered; the vegetation sparse; and water practically non-existent.

The mental picture which rises to the mind in thinking of a typical sheep-hunt is that of high Alpine meadows at ten to twelve thousand feet altitude, reached after long climbing through forests of pine and fir, surrounded by peaks carrying snow fields in their valleys and everywhere little rills of icy water threading the sheep meadows and tinkling down to join the streams below; meadows where the ptarmigan in their pied coats cluck and call their young.

The air is usually cool, if not wintry; the wind blows with violence and great fitfulness, to the despair of the patient stalker who, through a whole morning perhaps, has maneuvered to take advantage of it, only to have it turn against him at the critical stage. How different from what lay before us!—all except the wind!

Up at daybreak, we stowed away a hearty breakfast in our persons and a light lunch in our saddle pockets; slung three quart canteens on the shady side of our saddles, and a smaller one under the left arm; tied sweaters or leather coats behind the saddle; then rifles in scabbard, and field glasses about our necks, we mounted and rode slowly out of camp.

The air was sweet and fresh and our hearts were high with the joy of a new day, and our hopes for its fruition. The way soon left our ridge, crossed a big lava flow, where the horses picked their way with great care, then worked up between parallel walls of a ridge we could not cross, and so up and on to another bench; traversed a little flat, avoiding the thorny scrub all along the way; climbed a long sandy cinder hill, where the horses sank beyond their fetlocks; and so up, level by level, always up; light blue skies above us; keen, thin air in our nostrils.

By ten o'clock we were working up a rough valley under the shadow of the eastern peak amid strange manifestations of volcanic action, ridges which were hollow lava shells inflated by gasses from below, then left to cool in the likeness of grotesque distorted aqueducts — cones rising like spouts from whose ruined mouths we looked down dark unfathomed depths, out of which cool airs rose, and out of which falling stones brought us none of the very faintest and most distant sounds. In such a valley is Montezuma's House or cave and we dismounted to examine it. From the trail it was like a low barrel hill but clambering up we found ourselves on a rough roof of stones with a great ragged opening through which a small cottage might have been dropped and the sun shone down upon a floor thirty feet below.

On the far side it seemed possible to descend and as we approached the spot we saw a strange collection of short painted sticks from ten to twenty inches long and from ¾ inches to 1½ inches in diameter — the crude designs in red and black varied considerably as we came to examine them but all seemed to carry a religious significance. I knew that they were Papago Prayer sticks deposited by pilgrims to the House of the God by those who came to pray for rain, for healing, for all the simple needs of man — by Indians who had long since become outward Christians, yet still — or till very recently — sought the ancient shrine in a worship older than the New Testament.

Clambering down we explored the long cave with flashlights brought for the purpose, and in nooks and corners found other prayer sticks and ceremonial arrows, the latter far gone in decay.

The floor was deep in dry powdery dust and in a dark recess we found sheep bones, showing that cougar or wolf had made his lair here.

Leaving the cavern we rode on and soon the trail led through a perfect garden of the ugly cholla, which gave the horses much trouble.

Picking cholla burrs off the hind legs of a strange horse is quite a sporting proposition but must be undertaken; even the Mexicans did that, and I am glad to give them credit for the kindness. We used light pliers with which I always travel. They used a loop of bent brush, seizing the burr and holding it by pressure as of tongs.

Charlie's method of hunting was interesting to observe, and can only be accounted for by the plentifulness of game. As the lightest man, he led the procession, while I brought up the rear as the heaviest. We rode nonchalantly over ridges which I would have approached with great circumspection and peered over with caution, and Loretto's blue overalls and soiled light shirt were about as inconspicuous as a Holstein cow in a June pasture, so I concluded the sheep must be far away.

Habit is strong, however, and from my post at the rear, I kept a roving eye on the hillsides, bare except for occasional cholla which made bright white patches in the sunshine as did the low growing brittle brush.

We presently rounded a turn from which we looked past the shoulder of a low hill on our right, across a valley to the north slope of West Peak and, as I scanned its nearly barren side, I caught, low down near the base, a rather odd grouping of grey stones which arrested my attention, then aroused my suspicion.

Halting my horse I slipped the binoculars out of my shirt where they hung by the strap about my neck, gave one quick look at those "stones" set at odd angles, and then after a hiss, which arrested the man ahead of me, whispered sharply, "Sheep," slid to the ground and pulled my gun from the scabbard in one motion.

Charlie caught the signal, and my direction at once, was off his horse in a hurry, and leading us all quickly down to one side and out of sight in a draw, where we tied the horses.

Fearing the sheep might have seen us, the Mexicans were eager to get within close range before they started to move, so they ran down the slope, crossed the little valley, and began rapidly to climb the steep side of the opposite hill, which had screened us, and from whose top there should be good shooting.

I labored in the rear, my rifle, canteen, camera, and

glasses weighing a ton as I pushed up that slope. The hill was cinders, as bad as a sand dune, and even at that altitude, some 3,500 feet, my breath was scant after my run, so I was only half way up when they gained the summit, where a sort of natural wall, a rock outcrop, broken in spots, enabled them to look over without showing more than head and shoulders.

Keeping an eye on them as I climbed, I saw them in silhouette against the sky line raise their rifles, lower them, then turn and beckon excitedly to me. I was still laboring heavily up the slope, so fearing that the sheep had gotten our wind and were already in motion and to wait for me would spoil their chance, I signalled "go ahead."

Bang! went John's little gun, then bang went Bolton's bigger one, and kerack! kerack! went the Winchesters, then pumping and firing, the whole squad was in action too fast to count. Gaining the top ten seconds later I saw across a steep valley and some two hundred or more yards distant, the north slope of the ashy gray peak, green tinted toward the base with some herbage on which had been feeding and scattered over it the bounding figures of several sheep, whose sunlighted horns proclaimed them rams.

Just to be in the party, I fired at one as he mounted the skyline some six or eight hundred yards away, and had the pleasure of seeing the bullet kick up the dust under him, and then they were gone!

The creatures seemed smaller in size than their northern brothers and lighter, which I found later to be a fact, but the only specimens remaining to examine lay at the base of a little cliff and partly concealed even from my glasses by a bush.

After the excitement was over I learned that John had broken the hip of a good ram, his first shot, the beast turning as he fired, and Charlie Foster had then hit him and then John brought him off the rocks with a second shot forward.

I examined the animal carefully, noting its short coat of light tan and gray hair, with little or no fur beneath, its slender neck and legs as compared with the Wyoming sheep. The horns a dark amber color, very dry but not scaly, were well-proportioned and of good size, — 16½ inches at the base and running the full curve. Altogether a fine specimen, and worth the trip.

All of us were pretty well winded by the climb, though I suffered the most, but the Mexicans having skinned out the ram and shouldered the head, hide and meat, were now sliding and scrambling down the hillside, followed by small avalanches of cinders, leaving us to rest and enjoy alone the great view. Presently, finding that we were perhaps a quarter way up the peak, we decided to climb Pinacate on that very day, and set out on an easy jaunt toward the top.

John took the lead, his long legs carrying him easily up the steep ascent, while Bolton, who bore off to the right, kept fairly near him. I took a diagonal course to the left, steering safely between the cactus clumps and sinking to my ankles in the loose cinders at each step. I made a very laborious climb on the ascending spiral course, which finally brought me over the crest, to find my two partners seated on a small rock cairn, and admiring the truly beautiful view.

Heated by the climb, I had no sooner topped the crest than I felt the delicious relief of a cool moist breeze and the first sight greeting my eyes was the pale blue reach of bright waters — the Gulf of California.

There it lay below us, beyond the black lava ridges and gulches, beyond the wide belt of glowing yellow sands, a living sea of emerald and sapphire and at its further side the dim blue outlines of the mountains of Lower California. Weary from the climb, parched for water, I sat down beside the stone cairn with legs outstretched to rest them the better, and too much moved by the outlook for speech, I slowly tilted my canteen high, let the precious fluid go gurgling down my throat, and drank deep to the good Red Gods who had led us safely hither. Rain water, it was, taken from a not over clean tank, and all of a year old, but it was, in that place and then, a drink divine!

My eyes feasted on the distant blue water as, by judicious mouthfuls, I tasted to the full of the tiny store I carried at my side, and as I looked 'round upon the black basalt shining like iron in the sun, the cinder heaps more dry than words can picture, and across the burning plain to the north, where, thirty or forty miles away, was the peak under which was the nearest living water, I understood the dreadful danger of this region and the resource and wit of man who could so hold it at bay as to be able to venture into these vastnesses without disaster.

Turning to the cairn, we found tucked among the rocks two small cans, one square and rusted, the other cylindrical and not greatly affected by exposure. On prying off the top of the older one, it proved to contain the record of the ascent in 1907 of Dr. Hornaday, Professor McDugal and John M. Phillips. The paper was slightly stained with the rust but the writing was clear and legible, so we could note with interest that having spied some rams on the north slope Professor McDugal was about to descend and "collect" one. After trying for a photograph of it, we returned the paper, carefully closed the lid, and tucked it back among the stones. The second can held several visiting cards and leaves torn from notebooks giving the names of Charles Sheldon, the hunter-naturalist; Colonel John Greenway of the Calumet and Arizona, one of Roosevelt's close friends and a comrade in the Rough Riders; Dr. Rickert, the mining engineer; Benjamin Strong, of New York; Mr. Mills, of Washington, and several others.

We wrote a brief record of our trip, giving names and dates, and the statement of John's age — fourteen — which doubtless makes him the youngest hunter to climb the peak after killing a good ram on its slopes. This paper we added to the record, and after attempting a few kodaks, which proved wholly futile in recording the distances, we turned to the down-hill grade with great regret at having to leave such an enchanting eyrie, making our way slowly by another route to the northwest, where rocky outcrop gives much better footing either going up or coming down.

The next day I climbed along a rocky wall, not taking much heed of my footing as my eyes were seeking sheep, when a heavy stone turned under my foot and I was pitched forward, but by a twist partially recovered myself, coming down safe from a bad drop among the rocks below, but with the stock of my Springfield broken sharply in two at the trigger guard, as it bridged my fall between two boulders. My hand alone was bruised and having gathered my wits and bound the two pieces of stock together with a small length of adhesive tape I carried in my pocket for emergencies, I followed the ridge to its end, wishing to locate Bolton, whose rifle I had heard barking at such intervals as led me to believe he had scored a kill.

Sure enough, way out on a jutting point at a spot which overhung the gorge below, he had neatly dropped a fine ewe without a struggle, and we had the first specimen for the Carnegie Museum. He had made a perfect frontal shot at about ninety yards.

As before, we lunched in a tiny sand plain wedged in between two hills, where a mesquite tree about the height of a man on horseback gave us a little shade. At such times, Charlie and his son would squat over by their horses eating their lunch separately, and usually beside a little fire, on the coals of which they broiled strips of jerked sheep put up a day or so earlier. Their process of preparing this "jerky" was interesting to watch and they were usually at it late into the night, with a flaming big fire to light their operations.

The meat was cut in thin sheets, then into strips as wide as a man's hand, and salt rubbed into them, then having roughly stripped of its worst thorns the dozen or more whiplike branches of a convenient ocatello bush, they proceeded to impale these on the lithe limbs till the bush looked like an admiral's ship all flagged. The air and the sun soon dried these salted strips and it was then available as food, and Charlie was so industrious in accumulating a supply, which he seemed to regard as his particular property, that I had finally to give him direct orders to leave us enough for camp needs.

We usually went to sleep watching their figures busy against the firelight preparing this meat and waked in the early chill of dawn to see the new crop of "jerkey" blossoming on the ocatillo bush.

There is no doubt that one of Charlie's objects in coming on the trip was to procure a meat supply, and guessing that we would make no demur, he proceeded to make hay when there was opportunity. One feels rather at the mercy of a Mexican in that strange country where he alone knows the water and the trails and while Charlie rendered us good service and was on the whole a pleasant companion, he distinctly showed his disapproval of our meat-killing scruples.

His standards were so wholly different from ours that we could not hope that he would understand ours. How could a man who tells you quite openly that in one year he killed over ninety sheep in this region? "What did you kill so many for, Charlie?" I inquired. "For meat," was his answer.

Next day — March 26th — we moved camp and I mended my rifle stock with a nail and more tire

tape so well that I used it all the balance of the trip
without difficulty.

We had a long, bad climb up toward the peaks,
finding plateaus or benches covered with big lava
chunks, which made very hard going for the poor
horses whose hocks were cut in many places.

Seeing no rams anywhere we trailed some ewes and
lambs up over a bad hill to observe their place of retreat, but they seemed to have quite disappeared.
Bolton and John were exploring a high plateau of
small area when Bolton pointed out to the boy three
gray stones some hundred and twenty yards away and
below them saying, "You see how easy it is to mistake
a stone for a sheep," and as he spoke, the three stones
rose, got on their feet and became sheep before their
very eyes!

Both came hurrying to me saying here was the lamb
I wanted, and we all three lay down and wriggled
back over the rocks to where we could see the two
ewes and a lamb on their feet and looking in our direction. I bade them both try for the lamb and both
fired but without avail, and the sheep sped away like
race horses, the lamb in between the two older ones.
They ran down the slope and were crossing a gully to
mount the other side when, with a lucky shot, I
landed a Remington bronze point back of the baby
sheep's shoulder, and knocked him clear off his feet

without, however, killing him instantly, and John had to run down and give him the knife. He proved a good specimen, but I hope I won't need to get another little one for anybody.

We spent the next day out on the plain hunting antelope, and the following morning we put an extra blanket under our saddles, some meat and bread in our saddle pockets and with an extra large canteen, made our way up into the peaks for a two-day hunt and a night out up in the sheep beds.

After ten o'clock the day was warm. My pocket thermometer registered 115° as we rode across the plain the day before, but except for the sensation of a drying process going on in the skin and a narrowing of the eyelids against the glare of which even our wide hats were only a partial defence, there was no real discomfort.

The day's hunt was a grilling one for man and beast, for we covered a great "scoop" of country in our anxiety to locate rams, and our failure to do so was quite a blow to Charlie who ended the day quite low in his mind. He expected, I am sure, to find other bands as large as that seen the first day and our lack of success may have given him some glimmer of a conception that sheep are not inexhaustible but can be killed off by persistent slaughter in season and out. I hope so, anyway!

By noon we had scouted the third bench and could see the other side of the range and the Gulf, for we had climbed well though still on the east slope.

We lunched in the shade of the largest ocatillo we saw on this trip; that is, made up of the greatest number of stems, for we counted seventy-five in all, though this did not reach the height of a giant we had found growing in a tiny adobe plain in a natural rock garden near our first camp, whose stems we estimated to be fully 25 feet long.

Toward evening we located a camping place on a little flat near a curiously formed mound of rock bearing a miniature botanical garden on its crest. The horses were tied out to strong bushes where there was a little grass and scrub for them to nibble at, and we left them, glad to rest even without water, and only a few handfuls of barley apiece, while we arranged our bedrolls on the smooth earth floor and then, rifle in hand, we scouted some high ridges nearby for a possible sunset ram. We found none, but saw a gorgeous sunset over the Gulf and enjoyed a heavenly breeze blowing from it.

This was, we knew, our last real day of opportunity for sheep, and we were therefore not long over the breaking of our fast. The horses were stiff, but glad to be moving and we turned their heads west of north, riding at first and then leading them in rough places, skirting deep rifts or little canyons; climbing ridges; halting to scan hillside and plain, but finding only two or three ewes which grazed on a slope above us, not apparently greatly disturbed by our passage.

About nine-thirty we sighted two little piles or peaks set a hundred yards apart at the head of a depression which developed later into quite a gulch which fell eventually over a cliff down onto the plain. Charlie turned his horses toward them and presently dismounted, making his way on foot into a sandy gully, where he knelt, and after a moment's look around began to dig with his hands, throwing out the sand as does a dog in a hole. When I reached his side I saw he had uncovered a moist spot and by the time I had joined him in the excavation with John and Bolton moving further back the sand we threw out, there was a gallon or two of water shining in the bottom. We continued to dig until we had a small tub full, and lay down for a long, deep draught of the good cool water. A peculiarity of the Pinacate water is its complete freedom from the brackish or saline quality natural to most water, stream or well, in that region of the Southwest. This was one of those hidden tanks knowledge of which is traditional and known only to a few Indians and Charlie Foster, and the pool held enough to refill our canteens and give our horses all a long drink without unduly diminishing the visible supply.

There are some nine or ten such places, Charlie tells me, scattered over the volcanic area, but he is not disposed to give exact information as to their locations. We filled this one in again before we left — to prevent evaporation and to keep animals from fouling it — then took up again our long day's hunt over the crusted and inhospitable hills.

Working west and south, we made a very big circle mainly on lava benches and crossing ridges which run out west toward the plain, the roughest and most forbidding country we encountered.

Finding a rough way down, we at length descended into one of the deep gullies or little canyons which open to the plain till we were at an altitude of less than 1,000 feet above sea level, our night camp by my aneroid having been 2,900 feet.

In some of these wild gullies with their heated lava walls, there was good grass, for the soil deposit of the floor was in spots fertile and we occasionally found mesquite trees.

Our course lay across this system of canyons, so up and down we went with great labor and much of the climbing on foot with our horses in lead. One ewe and lamb we saw in a gully and then as we surmounted a long slope which ran like a rampart toward

the bench on which our overnight camp lay, John and
Charlie routed out two sheep that went ambling off
to our right, and our guide called back to my question, "Does?"— but as I pushed forward, I caught a
glint of horns, so slid out of the saddle pronto, calling to Bolton, who had not located them, to follow,
and ran to the edge of the little ridge over which they
had disappeared.

For once my agile partner was slow and before he
reached me, the last animal was on the brink of another jump-off, some three hundred yards away; and
just as I sat down to make ready for a steady shot if
the chance came, he leaped lightly to a little pile of
rocks on the very sky-line, a beautiful silhouette, his
four feet gathered under him, his back arched, and
even as I looked hard to appraise him, he turned his
head in full profile and I caught the beautiful outline
of his yellow horns shining in the sunlight, sweeping
backward and up in one majestic curve to the full
circle!

He was a young ram with a fine symmetrical head
— a worthy trophy — and I called to Bolton, "Shoot
him," turned my head to see why he did not, realized
that he had not yet located the animal, and decided
instantly to try myself, but as I looked back and
raised my rifle, the beautiful creature with a rocking
bound, dropped off his pedestal and disappeared into

the gully below — safe and unhurt! He was our last vision of the elusive, desert roaming Pinacate ram.

There was no trace of him — some side canyon had swallowed him up and with half regret half glad feeling that such a noble head was still alive — we made our weary way up the slope to our little camp. A pot of tea and some "jerkey" picked us up a bit but Charlie was morose and distant, sat apart from us and made a separate fire on the coals of which he boiled his mutton ribs which he ate in gloomy silence. We were in distinct disfavor — as meat-getters we had proven failures in his eyes and under that cloud we lived until our separation at the close of our desert sojourn two days later.

With blankets under our saddles we slung canteens and saddle bags aboard once more and at the end of a hard three hours' ride, mainly down hill, with our poor horses leaving blood trails on the rocks from their lacerated hocks and feet, we came to camp about 6:30 to find John Brown waiting, with a good savory stew and so our hunting for the Volcano Sheep was ended.

Photo by Prentiss N. Gray.

THE GREAT GLACIER ON THE STIKINE

CHAPTER X.

Three Days on the Stikine River

By EMORY W. CLARK

We had been up in the wilds of British Columbia hunting big game and when we came into Telegraph Creek on the 26th of September, 1920 the little town loomed up like a metropolis. A month earlier ten or twelve of us from all parts of the country had come up the river in a flat bottomed gas boat and separated with our outfits into the wilds. Telegraph Creek with a population of 150, Indians, half-breeds, and a handful of whites, was a real outpost "where the trails run out and stop." With a government official to settle all disputes among the inhabitants, a doctor, on a salary of $700.00 from the government, looking after their ailments — though due to his losing a case the Indians had small faith in him — and two outfitters, one a squaw man, doing a great business with the hunters who find their way up to this far away land of plenty, the list of town notables is told.

The first news we had was that our boat had gone — two days early — and we were stranded for a week at least with our coastline boat sailing the 30th and

229

our useless round trip tickets in our pockets. There was a rumor that the coast boat would be delayed in sailing but what was a rumor in this isolated spot! We stampeded the telegraph station and haunted it all afternoon, but as it was Sunday there were no results in spite of money and strong language freely used. Finally we faced the fact that there was nothing to do but take to open boats and trust to our own good luck and strength to make the mouth 160 miles below! For the Stikine River boils with a current of three to eight miles an hour with rapids all the way down and snags of tremendous size.

When I realized the situation I lost no time and found through the telegraph clerk an old Indian, Gordie Campbell by name, the best river man in the country. He was cutting wood a mile out of town with his partner, a white man, and they both stopped and came in with me. It was every man for himself now! We found four boats with rough hewn oars and made ready for business with the entire town out to see us, cheering parties off.

The first boat left Monday morning around eleven, amidst a general hullabaloo, with a man and his wife and two Indians. At two thirty, two more men with their Indians pushed off and we left around three.

Our scow, 22 by 4 feet and flat bottomed, was loaded with our duffle (lighter than it had ever been, for we had discarded much along the way, and even our slickers and the provisions were gone). Gordie, a wonderful type of old Indian, sat in the stern steering with his short paddle, leaving my friend and me with Gordie's partner to take our turn at the oars. We were soon sweeping down the river in the rapid current. In no time the old boat was taking water so fast we could hardly keep her bailed. Shortly after, we sighted a boat lying beached so we went ashore and changed crafts, but with little improvement.

It was a grand feeling going down that river with the current running nearly six miles an hour and the rapids boiling among cross currents. Great snags of fallen trees shook and quivered in the surge of water. In some places it was wide, with pleasant banks thick with ground-pine and fringed with willows; again sheer walls of black rock rose above the whirling waters and in places black volcanic rock slides reached down to the edge. It was nip and tuck, with all the speed we had, and Gordie on the watch, shifting his cud of tobacco to shout "Hoop — over we go!" or when we struck the rapids "Give her the gas!" The waves at times ran three feet high, curling and rushing into whirlpools that must be avoided when they are filling. It was terrific work rowing hour after hour in that thundering torrent! We must maintain our headway sufficiently for steering.

Near dusk we sighted the campfire of the fellows in the boat ahead and joined them for supper. We had a cheerful camp with a quarter of mutton from our last sheep for supper, and being worn out turned in early.

About three in the morning rain set in and by five we were up, but the Indians with the other boat were lazy, shiftless fellows and we were two hours getting under way. The rain was torrential, with a cold wind blowing up the river, and we were drenched in no time, city rain-coats giving no protection. We shot the rapids, bailing every little while and putting all we had into the oars. I shall never forget the wretched wet bag of potatoes I sat on between shifts — to row was more comfortable, and certainly warmer. At noon the other boat suggested tea ashore and we followed them. It was the sorriest looking crew imaginable huddled about the fire that Gordie had started with the help of kerosene; unshaved, drenched through and chilled to the bone with the biting wind, we would have passed for a bunch of the toughest roughs in the country! For a half hour we huddled about the meager fire trying to keep warm and lunching on bacon and tea, before we again took to the boats.

The rain continued in torrents all day and splashed into the leaking boat. Gordie said he knew of a deserted trappers cabin not over thirty miles down and anticipation cheered us on. What are thirty miles with shelter at the end! We reached where the cabin should have been at dusk, with the rain still pouring, and had difficulty in locating it. When we did, at a distance of about a hundred yards from the river, we found to our disgust that earlier high water had been up in it for weeks and the floor and walls were plastered with wet sticky silt.

We were completely exhausted, for the strain was telling on us. Gordie's partner, who had on only light cotton underwear and a blue jumper, was shaking like a man with the palsy. He was a husky chap, accustomed to twenty miles of traps in weather ten to fifty below, but the fourteen hours exertion in an open boat with a cold wind driving against his thoroughly soaked light clothing had done him in. One of the men had some whiskey and in a few minutes he was able to pull himself together, take off his shoes and stockings, get them on again and go to work bringing up guns and duffle from the boats.

Across the front of the cabin there was a covered porch about 12 by 6 feet and we built a fire in front of it with some boxes we found inside and the help of kerosene oil. Then we white men stripped, wrung our clothes and rubbed with partially dry towels from the outfit. It was a weird scene! The porch acted as a reflector for the fire and in the eerie light with the guns hanging up around and our clothing steaming over the heat, we supped — on lamb stew, tea and hot bread — and my, but it was good! Outside our shelter the rain still poured in the cold dark.

Conversation drifted back to the power boat that had failed us and the doctor in the party said he hoped the captain would need an operation and he'd officiate. Somebody wanted to administer the anesthetic but "Hell, no" said the doctor, "we wouldn't give him any!"

The Indians were tired, sullen and not of much use — we all were tired, too, but made ourselves as comfortable as possible and turned in early. It rained all night and when I awoke in the early dawn the Indians were still sleeping, stretched out on the porch beyond the smoldering fire. "Good God, boys, are you dead?" said Gordie waking them up. So passed the second night.

We left early, a villainous looking lot, through the mud and wet sagging bushes made our way to the boats, bailed and pushed out again! The rain had raised the river some nine feet during the thirty-six hours since we started, washing away great strips of the shore with many trees, and the snags had increased. Skirting the shore, in following the current, we saw bear and moose tracks all along, but they passed unremarked and failed to stir us! Where the

clouds lifted from the mountains we saw that the
waterfalls we had noticed on the up-trip were doubled
and trebled in foamy splendor, but the mood was
lacking to enjoy the glorious sight.

About noon a cheer went up from the other boat
whose passengers sighted a small tug tied to the
bank. Our hopes soared and the rain let up — but it
wasn't our boat at all! It belonged to the young
couple who had come down ahead and there wasn't
room for us all on board. They were going bear hunting thirty-six miles below on the Iskut River and they
asked us to drop down if our boat didn't arrive! So
we started on again, wearily.

In the afternoon the boat used by the government
for pulling snags picked us up. It was a gas boat and
they promised to make Wrangell, Alaska, before
dark. We had rowed some 120 miles and went aboard
with great cheer and made ourselves comfortable
about the kitchen stove. The last boat had not yet
caught up and we delayed for them as long as possible
but finally left, depending on a tug anchored near
there to see them through.

As we neared the mouth of the river, the fog rolled
in, obscuring the shore lines and with it came wind and
a high sea. Snags of two to four feet in diameter increased our danger and the channel spread out like
fingers over the mud flats. Only one dark bluff was

visibly outlined and we began scraping on the mud.

Up in the pilot house with the front glass down and the wet misting in, we sat around on the captain's bunk. The pilot in his slicker peered right and left for snags and the sea pounded us heavily. We would have gone to pieces in no time had we grounded and we were perilously near it. "Lord help us now boys, if we don't get out of this!" was all the Captain said. The propellers were raised into their sleeves, the Captain signalled for full speed ahead, and we went over.

The lights of Wrangell glimmered round the point and we continued on into the heavy seas but with the joys before us of a good hotel, dry clothes, good food and a chair to sit in.

We thought of the two long, lazy days spent going up river in the comfortable gas boat; when the beauty of the river thrilled us at each curve and game tracks, thick on the shore, were a never ending source of interest! We had seen the Stikine smiling and in her blackest moods and we felt, every one of us, that we knew her.

GIANT SABLE HEAD AND TOMÁ, THE GUNBEARER

CHAPTER XI.

Giant Sable Antelope

By CHARLES P. CURTIS

In September, 1923, my son Richard and his wife and I made a home camp in the Giant Sable Antelope country in Angola, Portuguese West Africa, between the Cuanza and the Loando rivers and near smaller tributary rivers, the Luce, Lucingé and the Tunda. We had travelled from Lobito Bay by railroad, by automobiles, and the last part of the way on foot with a safari of porters, greatly aided by the kind services of the Reverend John T. Tucker and his wife, of the Currie Institute at Dondi. We took no riding animals or oxen with us partly on account of the delay in getting them to the end of the automobile roads and partly because there are said to be tsetse fly in the sable country. A man's risk of getting sleeping sickness from the tsetse fly is small because, even in a sleeping sickness country, only a few flies carry the trypanosome germs but every tsetse fly can and will kill domestic animals.

We were to try and collect a specimen of this *Hippotragus niger variani,* an antelope that has until lately been a problem to naturalists ever since the 15th century, when a Portuguese adventurer brought to Florence a single sixty-one inch horn of an unknown animal; it is there in the museum now, much mutilated by scrapings that have been taken from it for medicine. Boer hunters have known the Giant Sable but it remained for Captain H. F. Varian, to whose hospitality and advice all sable hunters owe so much, to distinguish it in 1920 from the ordinary sable antelope by differences in skull formation and face markings, as well as by its longer horns. The British Museum recognized it as a new species, named it after Captain Varian and placed his specimens in the museum. The Giant Sable Antelope, *sumbakaloco* in the native language, with its long sweeping horns, its strong build and graceful poise is the handsomest antelope of them all; he stands about 4 feet 8 inches high at the shoulders and weighs about four hundred pounds. The species is not known to live elsewhere than in this part of Angola where we were camped, an area of perhaps 50 miles square. There are only a comparatively few specimens living and unless these get better protection than the Portuguese government is giving them the species will soon become extinct. Besides those that are being killed for specimens, many are killed by the native black hunters who offer the horns for sale for small sums. I have lately been told that one of our large museums sent an expedition to Angola to collect specimens of the female for their group, and that after three months they were unsuccessful.

Our camp was near a spring of good running water, and while no African water is really good until it has been boiled, it seems to be safe enough for the natives to drink without boiling, and a clear spring with plenty of water for everyone makes for a happy camp.

We had been correctly advised to bring everything with us because, in Angola, we would not be able to buy anything except sugar and flour; so we had brought to Lobito Bay from Capetown a good camp outfit, collected in the light of our recent East African experience and with the aid of a Newland Tarleton outfitting list from Nairobi. Our tents were made on a rush order by a sailmaker, and pots and kettles, food and bedding were packed in 50 pound padlocked porter's boxes, cross sectioned in the essentials, so that by the loss of one box we would not lose, for instance, all the salt or all the bacon.

We had spent six days in this camp, hunting in various directions, Richard going one way and I in another, when at last I located one evening two miles miles from camp, among the acacias, a herd of about twenty Giant Sable Antelope with at least one black bull. There hadn't been enough of the sunset left to stalk the bull and make sure of a shot, — near the equator the sun drops suddenly behind the horizon and the light soon goes with it, — so the gun bearers had suggested that it would be wise to wait till the morning; that probably the beasts if left to themselves would stay there for the night; that they would feed before moving off and that then we could track them through the grass moistened by the morning dew. So we had left them, and that night our alarm clock having got out of kilter, I went to sleep trying to get it fixed in the back of my subconscious mind that I must surely wake up before daylight and rouse the camp for an early start.

I woke up about four o'clock and pulled on my hunting clothes, i.e., a cotton undershirt and a brown woolen shirt and the old pair of blue serge trousers that I was going to offer as a prize. They were going to be a determining element in the success of our trip. The hunting costume of the country is whatever you happen to have, but the shoes ought to be good; my recent East African hunting had taught me that two pairs of woolen socks and light weight shoes were the best, and I had carefully selected them. I did not try any experiments with the African equatorial sun and so wore a Terai hat and a spine pad. A Terai hat is two broad brimmed felt hats, one on top of the other.

The thermometer showed 50° when I got up; it was always about that in the night, but I knew it was going to be 95° or more in the middle of the day so I wouldn't need any coat, I would go light. The porters and gun bearers were going to carry everything I wanted, gun, field glasses and water bottle. I put a few emergency cartridges in one trouser pocket with my raisins and cheese for lunch and in the other, my pipe and tobacco; and an extra undershirt, for it isn't wise in a malarial country to sit down wet in the middle of the day. I slipped on my winter overcoat until we started and found the party rejoicing in the coming of the seasonal rain in the night; it was going to make the ground moist and soft and the tracking good, and that's half the game in this parched country, baked by three rainless months of tropical sun. You have to depend on tracking to a large extent to find your game because, through the acacia trees you can't see much further than 300 yards ahead of you; that's not very far in a country where the game is scarce. My son and I, hunting separately, saw forty-four male, female and young Sable in a week of hard hunting from sunrise to sunset.

We had a good Capetown breakfast; stewed dried fruit, a cereal with condensed milk, canned baked beans, bacon and coffee; everything but bread. We had some rather weevily flour but no one knew how to make bread, not even the cook. We had no fresh meat because we had resolved not to fire a shot until we shot at a Sable, for fear of frightening the object of our hunt.

Richard and I joined forces for the day; I was to take the first shot but we hoped that there would be another black bull in the new herd for him to follow too. We started before daylight, Tomá and Augusto ahead with our guns; Richard had his Springfield 30-06 and I had my Holland and Holland 450, double express, that I had been using in Kenya for big game. It weighed eleven pounds and was unnecessarily large, no doubt, but I didn't have to carry it and I knew I wasn't likely to get more than one shot at the game we had come so far to kill. If I could get the shot, I figured that such a soft nosed bullet driven by cordite would stop him in his tracks if I could hit him somewhere near the right place. Even if he was not killed at once, the big bullet would give him the shock that stops even a bigger animal momentarily and then I would have a chance to shoot again. If I could hit him at all the blood would flow and we could track him more easily. A small bore rifle may kill as well as a big one in the hands of a good shot, but even the best shots — and I wasn't one — can't be sure; and a small bullet may make a wound that will close and prevent the flow of blood.

Alan Chapman, our excellent guide and interpreter was with us; he is a young Boer, a grandson of James Chapman, one of the old pioneering Voor trekkers from the South, a famous hunter who wrote an interesting book of old trekking and hunting days, *Travels in the Interior of South Africa*. Our Alan Chapman knew the native languages and Portuguese as well as English; without his aid our difficulties would have been multiplied. He has now in 1931 developed into the best guide and hunter in Angola and has recently collected for the Field Museum in Chicago the skin of an Angolan Sable Antelope with a sixty inch head.

Behind us all came some of Alan's excellent porters from his father's farm; we had collected our eighty-seven safari boys here and there; some from Lobito, some from the kindly helpful Plymouth Brethren Mission at Capango, but the strongest and best were from the Chapman home.

It was a large party that started out that morning, but all were keen and experienced and determined to win the rewards that I had offered and we planned to leave most of the porters behind when we got near the place where I had seen the herd the evening before.

We travelled fast before any signs of morning light had come — but not too fast, so as to avoid the pitfalls in the game trails that the natives dig to trap

the antelope, and hold them impaled on the sharpen-
ed stakes at the bottom.

Most of the sable country is as flat as a Colorado
plain; Angolan acacias about 25 feet high grow in
nature's irregular, but still even, way that is so hard
to imitate; it is easy walking through this orchard
looking country as the underbrush and dry grass are
burned by the native hunters in their August game
drives. We found the Sable tracks and followed the
herd, and Thomas (Tomá in Portuguese) saw them
first. He would, he had the most wonderful eyes that
I had seen in Africa. He and I left the others behind
and crept through the sand and moss and muddy ashes
of the burned undergrowth to the leeward of the
herd; most of them were chestnut red cows and young
males, but the black bull was there and we manoeu-
vred behind trees and the toadstool-looking ant hills
until he evidently had smelt or heard us and stood
erect looking in our direction. I put my sights up to
200 yards and, lying on the ground where I was,
squeezed the shot on to his shoulder longer and more
carefully than I ever had squeezed before; too long
for safety so Richard and Alan looking through their
glasses thought and said afterwards; but he stood
motionless until the shot had hit him at the point of
the shoulder a little higher than his heart and higher
than I had aimed; he reared until it seemed that he

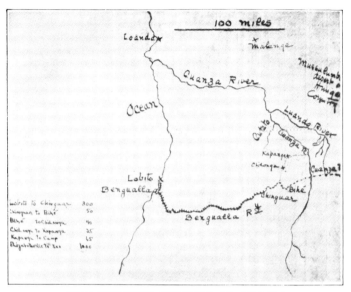

THE WESTERN PORTION OF ANGOLA

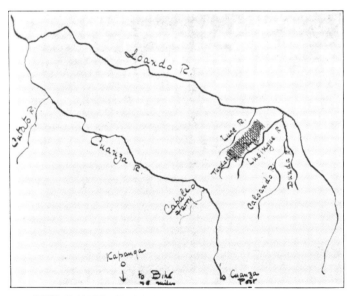

THE RANGE OF THE GIANT SABLE ANTELOPE

must fall backwards but gathered himself and ran plunging and kicking as I shot again and missed him; he was off with his cows around him. The first shot out of an oily barrel throws high and I was to have leisure, during our five hours chase, to repent that I hadn't run a rag through the barrel of my gun that morning.

We hurried to the spot where he had stood and found blood and as Richard had seen no other bull we all started on his trail together and began a morning of checks and perplexities; Tomà ahead, carrying in his left hand his old brown battered hat and in his right a long straw, picking gently here and there at the leaves and grass that seemed perhaps to have been disturbed by the wounded Sable. We blessed our good fortune that the rains had come; they had helped us to find the herd and now helped us to follow fast over the soft wet ground. A running Sable spreads his toes and leaves a deep track. But I can still remember the first hard rocky ground he had crossed; Tomá's first hesitation. I went back to the last definite sign where we had found a drop of blood and a fragment of bone, shoulder high on the leaves of a bush; I stuck a piece of paper on that bush to mark a certain starting point from which we could begin to track again. I might have been spared some of my feelings of disappointment and anxiety if I had known, as I know

now, Tomá's abilities as the best tracker of my African experiences. He had all the confidence and dogged patience of a beagle on the trail of a rabbit. I feel confident that the best tracking is done by an animal instinct that can't be taught and can't be described. It is this instinct as well as the sense of smell that enables a pack of stag hounds to pick out the tracks of their own hunted stag when crossed by another herd; it's an instinct born, that has been seen in a negro boy of ten who tracked better than his elders.

My experience had been that, while many natives could track well for a short time, the black man's brain does not let him concentrate for long. But Tomà's efforts never lagged. He is of the Ovinbundu tribe, the most intelligent of the West Coast blacks, the tribe that never came as slaves to our Southern States. They were known to be too intelligent and intractable to make good slaves themselves and so were employed by the slave traders to trail, capture and bring to the coast the natives of other tribes of the interior for export in the slave ships. Tomá was their worthy descendant; he knew and used the advantages offered. Our wounded Sable, for instance, went with the wind, perhaps intentionally, as then our scent would go from us to him and he could smell us and avoid us as we followed; but it helped us, too, because it gave the general direction in time of doubt.

The only aid I could offer were additional promises of new rewards. My offer of an axe and my old pair of blue serge trousers that I was wearing, soiled as they were by long use and creeping through the muddy ashes, had something to do with Tomá's tireless efforts. The axe had its effect but I thought I saw a new light of determination come into his eyes as he looked over my promised trousers and compared them with his own. If he failed, neither would Alan and Augusto get their prizes, and their speeches to him in the vernacular were, I knew, encouragement and prayers.

It was easy tracking through the occasional meadows where grows the mossy looking plant that is known to the natives as the food of the Sable; the food that is said to make the horns of the Angolan Sable grow larger than those of other Sables. It is possible that this is so, because this is the only species of Sable Antelope that feeds on it. The plant is not known in other parts of Africa; at least it is new to botanical science. Richard's wife, Anita G. Curtis, pressed it, described it and brought it home to the Gray Herbarium in Harvard University among other specimens of Angolan pressed plants. There it was found to be a new species and they named it *Cryptose-*

palum Curtisiorum. Welwitsch, a German botanist, "Catalogue by Hierni," and Baum, "Cunene-Zambesi Expedition," the best botanical authorities on Angolan plants and flowers, could not have come to this particular locality. The Sable country is one large malarial swamp in the rainy season; and perhaps they couldn't get there. They and other botanists have collected through most parts of Africa, but our Sable food plant had not hitherto been described, and at least it seems fair to assume that it is very uncommon.

Our Sable's own herd had soon left him to escape alone, leaving one single track to follow and that made our tracking more simple, but serious checks came when the tracks of other animals and even other Sable Antelopes had crossed his tracks; on other days we had seen roan antelope, oribi, reed buck, pigs and leopards and had been told that eland, puku, lechwe, waterbuck, and duikers live here. Tomá would motion us back so that we shouldn't step on the confused tracks and would search back and forth, studying the various conflicting foot prints, picking gingerly with his straw to see when the dust and dew had been disturbed; he always found the track again. Our Sable had left a trail somewhat different from others; even I came to know it. His broken shoulder caused his leg to swing out and around, and a dragging track resulted. I was becoming more and more confident as Tomá solved the successive problems but with the hot morning sun our difficulties were increasing; the dew and the rain of the night before were drying fast and the hard patches were left with few imprints. Tomá would circle these places and pick up the trail where our Sable had stepped on softer ground.

It was more important than ever not to make any noise, so we left the porters far behind to trail us, while Richard and I with our gun bearers followed Tomá silently on the trail. No one could help the cackle of the startled guinea fowl, but we tried not to deserve reproachful looks from Tomá and stepped carefully over the twigs and the parched and curled leaves, for the end would come as soon as one of us two could steal up for a finishing shot.

This day seemed to us to be particularly dusty, and thirsty, as the tropical sun got up over our heads. We had attempted to anticipate the thirst of the day by drinking all the boiled water we could before leaving camp and we were going to drink again at night, but with the walking and the intermittent disappointments and hopes I got down to the end of my water bottle. I filled it once at a stagnant pool in a meadow putting in a Halizone tablet used in the war and guaranteed by our friend Dr. Richard P. Strong to kill every form of microscopic life without killing us. As a matter of fact I put in two for good measure, it made the water bitter but it was wet. Any one who has been thirsty feels sympathy for the troops at Gallipoli; all the water had to be brought there in ships and they fought in the trenches of those hot hills on one and one half pints of water a day.

It kept running in my mind that we had to go back to the coast soon and if we didn't get this Sable we were going to fail as many other hunters of the Giant Sable had failed. I had roused this neighborhood with my loud cordite shots, but, above all, this flat low Sable country, with the coming of the seasonal rains that were beginning, was about to become a muddy swamp; an anopheles mosquito breeding marsh. We had been at this camp for a week and it was certain that the local mosquitoes had taken our porters' malarial germs that some natives always carry in their blood; the mosquitoes would have developed the germs by now and could bite them into us. Wise travellers move once a week to camps where their own safari germs have not been sown.

We were grateful, however, for the absence of the pests of the Canadian forests and streams; there were no gnats, black flies and other biting curses that make the life of the hunter and fisherman miserable. Even the Angolan mosquitoes allow you peace in the day and you can hide from them under your mosquito netting at night. They often kill with their malarial germs and they make most people very ill sooner or later, but they are not intolerable biting nuisances. You can bear the harmless Angolan flying ants that crawl but don't bite; they are among the few African insects that have not as yet been convicted of carrying the germs of some illness.

And we did not have snakes on our minds. Although we were told that there were mambas, cobras and puff adders, I had seen only one snake that I remember, an innocent chocolate colored boomslang that had been killed with enthusiasm by our porters.

I got the impression that there are not many birds in the country though we saw a few. I recollect a night jar with one long white pennant-looking feather at least a foot long fluttering from each wing.

Everything has some end, including the vitality of a Sable Antelope; he was going more slowly and we found places where he had lain down and had jumped again and run when we got near.

We had been warned to take care when we got near him; they have been known to kill dogs with sweeps of their scimitar-like horns; and even leopards are wary of the Angolan Sable Antelope. The upper part of their horns curve outward with a purpose, and the leopard that jumps on a Sable Antelope's shoulder and reaches for his nose to break his neck will be stabbed by a backward thrust for the spreading horns will pass over the antelope's own shoulders.

He was walking slowly now and the end came when Richard hurrying round to head him finished him with a heart shot.

We were all too tired to follow inclinations to shake hands and congratulate each other, but I saw on the tired dusty faces evidences of my own satisfaction; and to Richard and to me the long trip and the hard hunt with the successful end had made our trophy all the more valuable.

Richard shot a similar bull the next day, and full of gratitude to the rains that had come to our aid we travelled back to the coast leaving with regret Tomá, who waved his friendly farewell to us in the car window the morning we left and said his only English words, "Good night."

BEAVERS AND THEIR LODGE

CHAPTER XII.

Days With a Beaver Trapper

By HENRY T. BANNON

In "A Naturalist's Voyage," Darwin says that if
the love of the chase is an inherent delight in man —
a relic of an instinctive passion — he is sure the pleasure of living in the open air, with the sky for a roof
and the ground for a table, is part of the same feeling; that it is the savage returning to his wild and
native habits. Gilbert White, in "Natural History of
Selborne," says that it is impossible, even by penal
laws, to extinguish the inherent spirit for hunting in
human nature. It was this inherent delight, or inherent spirit, that led me to go hunting with a beaver
trapper. My experience and observations have increased my admiration for the beaver, and have enabled me better to grasp what I may read touching
this subject. Much has been written concerning the
beaver and his ways; his relation to discovery and
exploration, and his influence upon the development
of America have been duly recorded.* It was beaver

*Lewis H. Morgan, The American Beaver and His Works(1886)
Enos A. Mills, In Beaver World (1913).
Vernon Bailey, Beaver Habits (1922), Bulletin 1078 U. S.
Department of Agriculture.
Charles Eugene Johnson, The Beaver in the Adirondacks
(1927), Roosevelt Wild Life Bulletin.

fur that lured the early explorers into the unknown land west of the Alleghenies, along the streams that have their sources upon both sides of the Rockies; also, into Canada and the wilderness north to Hudson's Bay. What followed in the wake of these explorers is well known to history.

In regions easily accessible to man, beaver are readily exterminated; therefore, wise legislation has limited the areas in which they may be taken. In territory, where beaver trapping is permitted, the open season is also limited to certain periods. Such limitation maintains the supply. My observations were made during an open season upon mountain rivers in northern British Columbia. Those rivers, with their whirlpools, rapids, glacial silt, and the bird life that abounds along their courses, recall Virgil's description of the Tiber:

"With whirlpools dimpl'd; and with downward force
That drove the sand along, he took his way,
And rolled his yellow billows to the sea.
About him, and above, and round the wood,
The birds that haunt the border of his flood;
That bath'd within, or bask'd upon his side,
To tuneful songs their narrow throats applied."

I entered upon the trapping grounds in the spring as soon as the warm suns had released the streams from their icy coverings. There I found a new life, a new world, and a new people. The trapper and I ascended the Stikine River to Clearwater River in Cassiar, upon which he intended to close the trapping season, which ended May fifteenth. On our journey we passed several trapper's camps. The men were a sturdy, happy lot, living in various modes. Some lived in tents, others in little log cabins built for use only during the trapping seasons, and one outfit was sheltered merely by a wickiup. All had small boats and some had dogs that had brought supplies over the ice and snow to the trapping grounds. There were sourdoughs, who had not been outside for a quarter of a century; there were men who had been in the first line trenches in France; there were prospectors trapping for a grubstake and there were Indians and halfbreeds. Their camps were strung along the river for more than a hundred miles. There was a spirit of most friendly rivalry among them; and each outfit that we met on our way upstream wished to know how many skins had been stretched by those below. The future market price was also a subject of much serious conversation. Each was ready to help the other, and all were willing to extend hospitality to me. Their resourcefulness in contending with the forces of nature calls for one's highest respect.

During eras of excessively high prices for fur,

British Columbia wisely prohibits beaver trapping. The temptation even to exterminate is obvious. Convertibility into easy money is the most destructive enemy of the fur-bearer. During a closed season I was in this same region. The few trappers then there were those who had gathered their winter's harvest of marten, mink, fox, and lynx and were waiting the opening of navigation. Feathered game, such as geese, ducks, and grouse, was very tame because not persistently hunted. With the presence of many beaver trappers, however, I found such game to be both wild and wary; for the beaver trapper lives off the land. The trapper and the prospector believe, and they are right, that game is for their use; and that domestic animals are for the use of the man of the settlements and the cities. Consequently, the trapper knows no game law and kills as his necessities require. The city hunter kills for trophies of the trip, but the trapper kills for food. The one kills for show, the other kills for use. The Indian at such remote places as Liard Post fails to obey regulations prohibiting the killing of beaver. He brings them to market in spite of a prohibitory law; for they secure for him food, blankets, and traps. The provincial government was practically under necessity of buying the Indian's catch during the closed season, and this it did, paying ten dollars for a large skin and five dollars for a small one. They were worth much more, but to pay their value would increase the Indian's catch without any appreciable benefit to him, for invariably the Indian wastes his surplus funds.

Our permanent camp was on the shore of a cold glacial torrent; a wild stream that wound its course through a valley, one to two miles in width. The valley floor was of boulders and sand, ground from the mountains by the irresistible power of the hard ice. In flood time the torrent cut new channels at the bends, and the old ones became sloughs containing quiet waters. When the wind blows, great clouds of stinging sands sweep over the valley like driving sheets of rain in a summer storm. Cottonwood and willows line the sloughs and grow in extensive, but scattered, flats throughout the valley. The inner bark of these trees is the food of the beaver.

To trap beaver successfully, the trapper must understand the nature and the ways of this cunning animal. In such knowledge my companion was expert, and he was consequently successful. During the season he caught more beaver than did any other trapper within a radius of a hundred miles of his cabin. No craft is more interesting than that of the trapper. He must match his wits against the cunning and the wary. Perforce he is a naturalist. The trapper's thoughts each morning are woven about his luck for the day;

the pot of gold at the end of his rainbow. Hope, the hope of the capture of that which brings the daily bread, springs eternal on the trap line.

Beaver either live in the banks of streams and feed upon the bark of trees and brush along their shores; or they live in lodges that they build in ponds, and feed along its shores and upon the brush growing in the ponds. The ponds are the result of beaver built dams extending across running water; and the heighth of the dam governs the water level of the pond.

An abandoned and drained beaver pond afforded much information; for there the beaver's floor plans were laid before me. This dam was about nine feet in heighth and seventy-five feet in length. The side that faced the pond was of mud, while the side that faced down the stream was of sticks. The dam was bow-shaped, curving with the flow of the water. The area of the pond comprised from twelve to fifteen acres with little canals radiating through it. It is over these that the beaver carries the branches and twigs that he uses for food, for lodge building, and for dam repairs. The canals also afford sufficient depth of water to enable the beaver to submerge and take refuge from such enemies as wolverines, wolves, and bears. The side of each canal was as smooth as though cut with a spade, and free from projecting roots and other forms of obstruction. There are no snaggy bends in the canals upon which the beaver plies his work. There were two old lodges, both of which had been dug into by bears or wolves. This pond had been abandoned because all the food had been cut from it, or had been killed by the formation of the pond. The standing trees were dry with roots well rotted. The silt deposited during the life of the pond was a black rich looking loam, undoubtedly fertile for such hardy vegetables as will grow in this climate. From this object lesson, I could learn the value of beaver to mankind. Here was a spot made useful for man by the patient toil of this animal. The beaver had bestowed his labor on a piece of thin land, covered with useless willows, alders, and cottonwoods. He had destroyed such growth so thoroughly that no great amount of labor was required to fell and burn the standing trees and grub out their roots. By the same process the beaver has made many a rich meadow and field upon which the flocks and crops of man now flourish. No one can say, with any assurance of accuracy, that this old, abandoned beaver pond in northern British Columbia is useless because people do not dwell there. Should some extensive deposit of mineral be discovered in that region, this pond will be utilized as a garden spot to aid in feeding those who develop the mine. As such, it will be precious indeed. Should man not use it, it will again grow up in willow, alder, and cottonwood, and again will the beaver repair his dam, build new lodges, and occupy that which, in working for himself, he has made useful for man.

In good beaver country one will see smooth, worn, rising paths leading from the stream to the top of the bank. Such paths are known as slides, and are used by beaver in going to and from feeding grounds and to their soiling places; for they have regular places upon which to soil. During the spring and summer, beaver come out about twilight, or a little before, and remain out during the night. They will cross over the dam to the creek below and travel up and down the slides. These habits were the trapper's guide in setting his traps. One evening we put out in the canoe and set six traps, five of them being at slides and one at a dam. The latter was set on the pond side of the dam, at a place where the signs indicated beaver were accustomed to cross. Great skill is required to set a trap. Two objects must be accomplished; not only must the beaver be caught, but he must either be drowned or the releasing of the leg from the trap must be rendered impossible. If the beaver can do so, he will wind the trap chain around driftwood until he is able to break the bone in his leg and twist the leg off. His ability to set a trap properly is the measure of the trapper's success. I was told of an inexperienced trapper whose catch for one season consisted of three beaver and seventeen feet.

Picture in your mind a straight, smooth slide up the bank of a stream. It gives every indication of frequent use. Boughs overhang the bank. After noting such favorable conditions, the trapper gets a piece of driftwood or cuts a bough two or three inches in diameter and eight or ten feet long. This is known as a clog. He ties one end of the clog to an overhanging limb; to the other end he fastens the trap chain by half hitch and drops that end into the water. The trap is then set in the water at the foot of the slide, at a depth of about five inches. Stakes are driven at either side of the trap for the purpose of inducing the beaver to pass directly over the trap. Two or three willow twigs or a cottonwood stick from which a beaver has partially removed the bark, are laid on the slide for bait; the scent used by the trapper is also employed. To make this scent, my companion put a beaver castor into a bottle and covered it with alcohol or rum. When he set his trap, he dipped a small twig into this viscous substance and stuck it into the ground near the trap. A beaver swimming in the stream either intends to go up the slide or is lured to it by the bait or scent. He turns toward the slide, passes between the stakes, reaches the shallow water, steps on the trap and is caught. At once he makes for deep water or the current. The clog springs back and forth as he struggles, and holds him under the water until he is drowned. If a stone weighing about twenty-five pounds is wired to the lower spring of the trap, thus weighting it down, the beaver will drown more quickly. However, should there be a log nearby, the beaver will get over it and twist off his leg at the trap and be lost. The circumstances under which a trap is set necessarily vary, and the plan above outlined was modified as the circumstances required. It may be interesting to note that Lewis and Clark used the same scent as a lure, except that they added a nutmeg, twelve or fifteen cloves, and thirty grains of cinnamon, all pulverized together. Audubon found the same bait in use on the upper Missouri in 1843.

The morning after we set the traps we found three beaver caught and drowned. One was unusually large, weighing about sixty pounds, and the others were of average size which is from thirty to forty pounds. The tail of the large one was six and three-fourth inches in breadth. The beaver were taken to camp and skinned; the hides were dressed by removing the fat; then they were stretched on a tree that stood in the shade. To care for a large beaver skin properly requires an hour and a half's work by an expert trapper. The hindquarters of the beaver, and also the liver, my companion cooked. Beaver meat must be thoroughly disguised before I can eat it. The hams resemble duck legs, and while cooking they have the odor of fish. I cannot agree with those writers who refer to beaver meat as a delicacy, and better than roast pig. However, I have no doubt that I could acquire an appetite for beaver meat just as Stefansson and his men relished boiled seal.

Another way of taking beaver is by shooting them. This is exciting sport and, when the hunting is from a canoe, calls for better marksmanship and more skill than anything that I know of. But should the hunter take his place on the bank of a stream, alongside a tree against which he can rest his rifle, shooting is not so difficult. Toward evening, portage your canoe over a beaver dam into a pond and, rifle ready, watch for the appearance of game.

The restful sounds of evening claim attention. A tiny bird, that scolded when you first came, as though resentful of your presence, soon sings his best song from a bush on the mountain side; the robin carols a good-night. The ruffed grouse drums in the thicket and the shy varied thrush sends forth his plaintive cry from the depths of a wilderness. A pair of teal on their honeymoon, the groom arrayed in feathers now wearing their most gorgeous hues, comes to within two rifle lengths of your canoe and then they swim away unalarmed. The sun has sunk behind the range of ice and snow, but the afterglow illumines the mountain peaks; their whiteness is reflected in the waters, and a bright twilight is cast all around. All is still, save for the roll of the distant river and the roar of an occasional snow slide far up the mountains. Yonder a ripple is seen on the surface of an arm of the pond, and you know that a beaver is coming. He swims silently, his body covered by the water and only that part of his head above the nose and eyes is visible. Though he has seen you, curiosity is his master, and he continues slowly to draw near. You raise your rifle to shoot; you are too quick. Your sudden movement alarms the beaver, and down he goes. Instead of the report of your rifle, you hear the derisive plash of the beaver's tail; or you may shoot too late and hear both shot and plash. You should have raised your gun slowly; very, very slowly. There should be no quick movement of arm, hand or head. Another difficulty may be that the beaver is moving, your canoe is also moving, or is unsteady; and the mark is very small. Well, if you hit it, you are lucky. Then you must make haste to recover the animal; for, unless very fat, he will sink.

And thus I put in the time until the close of the season. The traps were examined each morning, and the sets made; the skins were prepared in the afternoon; and in the evening there was canoeing into ponds and sloughs. Something new ever arrested my attention, and I was happy. I learned much about beaver and about the life of a trapper. Trapping is hard work; but the season is short, being from October to May. A good trapper will have cabins convenient to his trapping grounds. Early in the season he must pack in the necessary supplies. For such purpose the canoe is unexcelled. One man can transport five hundred pounds of freight up a swift mountain stream at the rate of eight miles per day. The trapper's fare is simple; for, like the animals he seeks, he eats to live instead of living to eat. Oatmeal, hotcakes, moose (if he can get it), potatoes, beans, beaver-saddle and liver, canned milk, tea, coffee, and sugar constitute his bill of fare. Of traps, twenty-five are required for a good beaver line. As a trap, with chain, weighs about seven pounds, the labor of carrying several requires strength. Some who have told the story of John Colter's thrilling escape from Indians on the Jefferson Fork of the Missouri in 1809 intimate that it was foolhardy in him to return later to the scene of his adventure for the purpose of recovering some beaver traps that he had cached. There was nothing strange about it, however, for to John Colter the loss of his traps was a serious matter and possession of them was a real necessity. There was no trading-post nearby at which he could have replaced them; and when traps or food have been transported for more than a thousand miles, by man-power alone, and cannot otherwise be replaced, they are very valuable. John Colter did only what any other trapper of his time would have done under the same circumstances. The trapper of today must have his caches of traps, nails, and other imperishable necessities just as did the western trapper of old.

Beaver trapping early in the spring and late in the fall entails much personal exposure. In October and November, the weather is bleak and cold; ice forms on paddle, pole, and line. Rain, sleet, and snow chill the blood. In March and early April, there are snow, slush, and cold with which to contend. Nevertheless, a trapper with twenty-five traps on his line must make his rounds; must re-set sprung traps; and must establish new locations. Two beaver a day from such a line is an excellent average. The trapper returns to his cabin, wet and cold; the meal must be cooked; the catch skinned; the hides well scraped of their fat and stretched to dry. Often it is late in the night before the trapper turns into his bunk for a short rest until day breaks.

I think one will have greater success trapping in the fall than in the spring. During the fall, beaver are busy animals. They are at work laying up their winter's supply of food. They come to the bank of the pond or the stream, climb up the trails, cut willow or cottonwood sticks, carry them to the water, and then swim with them to the cache near the lodge. The cache is in the water. To make it, the beaver first plant a few sticks in the mud for the purpose of forming an obstruction. This done, they bring hundreds of branches and twigs and release them so that they will catch against those in the mud and become inter-woven. The ice finally covers the water, but the beaver's food is beneath the ice. During the winter, a beaver goes from the lodge to the storehouse, cuts a branch from the cache, returns to the lodge, eats the bark, and then puts the peeled stick into the current, which carries it away. While laying up their food for winter, beaver work earlier in the evening and later in the morning than they do in the spring. They are then very active and frequent well established places; and the chances for their capture are better.

All beaver trapping should cease by May first. April fifteenth would be better, as the young are born the latter part of May or early in June. Yet trappers, on navigable streams, will trap until the arrival of the first boat upon which they can be taken out. This is usually about May fifteenth; consequently that date closes the season. In May the catch is sold, usually to Hudson's Bay Company, or to some well established trader. If the tourist from the city wishes to buy, he must pay double the price paid by the trader, or not buy at all. There is good reason for this; for it is to the resident trader that the trapper looks for credit again and again. A reasonably diligent trapper will make more money than will a farmer owning a quarter section of good land. His catch will average about fifteen hundred dollars a year, and five hundred will keep him. But, like all the rest of mankind, practically every trapper is extravagant and his money is spent all too soon. Occasionally one will practice Thoreauean economy, and accumulate a competence sufficient to maintain him through middle life and old age.

Many incidents connected with beaver came under my observation. I noticed that the teeth of trapped beaver were invariably broken. They do this in gnawing the trap or chain. A strange noise, such as is made by striking the canoe with the paddle, or by casting a stone into the water, will often call beaver from their lodge in the daytime. Once the trapper tapped his gunstock three or four times with a knife. In less than a minute a beaver emerged from his lodge and swam about until he saw us; then he returned into the lodge. The water was clear, though deep, and we could plainly see every movement as he came out and swam about. Of course, the entrance to a beaver lodge must be beneath the water. Upon another occasion we were near a lodge located in a pond whose waters were not clear. Again, the same noise was made. After waiting several minutes, and neither beaver nor ripple appearing on the surface, we turned to go. As we did so, there was a plash a few feet in our rear. The beaver had come through a little underground canal to a small pool near where we stood and had evidently been watching us all the time.

The caprice of fashion was the principal cause for the early slaughter of beaver; and it was the caprice of fashion that stayed the hand of extermination. The hats of our great grandfathers were made of beaver fur, and such hats were in great demand both in Europe and America. That sometimes droll, some- times pathetic, poet, Thomas Hood, wrote:

> "*The Quaker loves an ample brim,*
> *A hat that bows to no salaam,*
> *And dear the beaver is to him*
> *As if it never made a dam.*"

It was to supply skins for making hats that the great trading companies entered into a competition remark- able for its intensity. After several years, beaver hats were displaced in fashion's favor by silk hats and the beaver ceased to be an object of pitiless persecution. Later, nutria (which is the fur of the coypu, a South

American animal somewhat resembling the beaver) came into use for various purposes and divided the burden borne by the beaver.

Lewis and Clark reported that beaver existed in multitudes at the head waters of the Missouri. All sportsmen have read with interest accounts of the methods employed which almost exterminated the buffalo, the antelope, the elk, and the mountain sheep. Why should not a reliable account of the expeditions of the beaver trappers of old be equally interesting and instructive? What methods were employed to deplete the multitudes of beaver seen by Lewis and Clark? In that intensely interesting work of Alexander Ross, "The Fur Hunters of the Far West," one may read an account of the author's experience while leading a beaver trapping expedition during the winter of 1823-4. This expedition hunted in Idaho on the Pacific side of the continental divide. The many incidents of adventure faithfully and simply recorded in this book make it one that every sportsman should read. In this article I can give only a summary of the hunt and an outline of the personnel of the expedition.

Ross was a representative of Hudson's Bay Company. He set forth in November with a motley band of fifty-five men, only twenty of whom could be considered trappers. There were two Americans, seventeen Canadians, some half-breeds, and the remainder Indians from various tribes. The outfit of each member was fixed by his ability to trap, or by the work he was to perform. The Indians were chiefly useful in caring for the horses. From five to ten of the white men were always on duty to guard against surprise from hostile Indians. The married men brought their families along, so that in addition to the men, there were twenty-five women and sixty-four children. The equipment consisted of seventy-five guns, two hundred and twelve beaver traps, three hundred and ninety-two horses, ammunition, clothing, and trading goods. The hardships endured by this band, while crossing the mountains, were severe; and the danger of attack by hostile Indians was almost a constant menace. It was not until April that they arrived upon the hunting grounds.

In the pass where Lewis and Clark had crossed to the Columbia, the Ross expedition took ninety-five beaver during the morning and twenty more during the remainder of the day. Upon one occasion they made a cache of one thousand beaver skins. Upon arriving at the extremity of the journey, Ross found that he had accumulated 3880 beaver. The party had traveled in daily journeys 1320 miles, upon trapping excursions 1110 miles, scouting for enemies 490 miles; searching for passes and new trapping grounds

530 miles; or in all 3450 miles. The men continued to trap and Ross states that at the close of the season his twenty trappers averaged 250 beaver each and procured in all 5000 skins. This he seemed to consider a reasonable result. I am not sufficiently well informed to speak accurately, but I think that any trapper who is at present able to capture fifty beaver during an entire open season has done unusually well. The details given by Ross are interesting. Trapping down Reid's River, the party took from seventy to eighty beaver each morning. Upon that expedition they obtained 1855 beaver. In three days, six men caught one hundred and fifteen beaver. During several successive nights the average catch was fifty-five. Some skins were acquired in barter. The Indians had no appreciation of the value of beaver skins and would sell one worth twenty-five shillings in London for a brass ring not worth a farthing. It was some time before the Indians woke to the realization of the fact that an article of barter of no value to an Indian might be of considerable value to a white man. It took 154 horses to convey all the skins to the outfitting point. The party lived on the game killed by the hunters.

It is not strange that, with such expeditions in constant pursuit, beaver soon became rare. In the early days about 200,000 skins were exported annually. The wonder is that any beaver were left. Audubon found them very scarce on the upper Missouri in 1843. In his work on the "Quadrupeds of North America" he records that a good trapper formerly caught about eighty in the autumn, sixty in the spring, and upwards of three hundred during the summer. But at the time that work was written (1842-6), he was of opinion that a trapper in the Rockies, who secured one hundred skins during the winter and spring, was fortunate. The presence of beaver in regions where the land is cultivated is adverse to agriculture. They are also a source of damage where timber of value is sparse. However, there are abundant expanses in the West, in Canada, in Alaska, and even in New York and Pennsylvania, where beaver should increase without injury either to the works of man or to forests valuable to man. When they become sufficiently plentiful to threaten valuable forest growth, they may be readily reduced to reasonable numbers. They increase rapidly, the annual litter being from four to eight.

Formerly beaver skins sold by the pound. Audubon learned, so he tells us in his "Missouri River Journal," that seventy average beaver skins weighed one hundred pounds and were worth five hundred dollars in a good market. This is a little more than seven dollars each. According to Ross, his rivals offered white trappers five dollars per skin and they were worth seven dollars and a half in the London market. Baillie-Grohman wrote that in the early eighties four dollars was considered a good price. During the first year or so of the great war many were sold at this figure, though the average price had been from eight to ten dollars each. In 1922 Hudson's Bay Company paid an average price of about sixteen dollars each. The size of the skin, weight, color, and condition of the fur are the elements entering into the value.

That they have not been exterminated in the United States is explainable only by the fact that their litters are large. Some of the western states now afford means for lawfully taking beaver for propagation. The applicant must have suitable range for them, such range being either a pond, or a stream that the beaver may dam to create a pond, and proper food supply of grasses, aspen, and willow. Such favorable locations abound in places where beaver are now unlawfully captured. Whether ownership of beaver on private lands will produce profitable results remains to be seen. It was to capture beaver for such an enterprise that I once set out with two men from a Montana ranch.

For several miles we traveled on horseback over a range where not long ago deer, elk, antelope, and buffalo abounded. The only wild life we saw was one jack rabbit and one coyote. It all seemed so desolate.

The packhorse bore the trap made in accordance with Vernon Bailey's design for a heavy trap to capture beaver alive. It was set late in the afternoon, on the arm of a lake, at the foot of a slide which gave every indication of recent and frequent use. Water grasses were strewn over the trap to conceal it. It lay at a depth of about four inches in order that the beaver would be wading when he entered it, thereby making it certain that he would strike the pan controlling the trigger; also to insure against the drowning of the captive. Some fresh aspen boughs were laid on the bank and beaver scent dropped along the slide.

Crossing the arm of the lake, we climbed the bank opposite the trap to watch. Towards dusk a beaver swam across the arm of the lake and disappeared from our view. Again it appeared, this time swimming silently and steadily along the shore where the trap was. Through binoculars her ears and black, beady eyes were plainly seen. How still and tense we were as the beaver neared the trap. How disappointed were we when she passed by. Such thrills when she turned, lured by the scent, and swam straight for the slide, entered upon the trap, stopped for a moment and then went on. The trap flashed shut amid a shower of spray. Down the mountain side we went, into the boat, and to the trap. There was our beaver, taking capture like the philosopher a beaver is. True, she tried to get her head between the chains but she was quiet and not disposed to make any scenes. No longer free, she made the best of it. We transferred the beaver from the trap to a side-pack, balancing the opposite side with some rocks, and set off for her new home. No pain had been occasioned to the animal, no leg crushed or broken, the teeth intact, not even a guard hair ruffled. We mounted our horses, rode out of the canyon in the twilight and over the sage brush for camp.

Despite the books on natural history, and the articles in magazines correcting the fanciful imaginations of the early travelers, the uninformed still attribute to the beaver many habits that make up no part of the life of that animal. Some of them it may be well to enumerate. Beaver do not use the tail as a trowel; neither do they use it for the purpose of carrying mud or stones. The tail is used in swimming; as a support on land; and as a means of giving a danger signal, both on land and water. The mouth is used to carry sticks; and mud and stones are carried by the forepaws. Beaver do not eat fish; they are strictly vegetarian, living on the inner bark of certain trees, on grass, and on some bulbous plants. Beaver never gnaw through a leg caught in a trap; they will, however, twist the leg off if they can get the trap wound around a log or a stake. Many writers are in error concerning this habit. Beaver do not know how to fell trees into a location best adapted to their purposes. Beaver cannot remain under water more than a few minutes; they breathe air, travel on land and in water, and they are not predaceous. Beaver castoreum, a substance contained in beaver castors, is no longer valuable as a medicine. Formerly it was used as a stimulant and as an antispasmodic; but better remedies have displaced it. Castoreum is now used in the manufacture of perfumery. The average price for large castors is from seventy-five cents to one dollar.

In canoeing from our camp to the mouth of the Clearwater, the skill of my companion afforded, in safety, fifty miles of thrills in five hours. In the hands of the expert, that is one who can, under the stress of all conditions, read the strong waters, know what to do and how to do it, the canoe is safe. But in the hands of the unskilful it is dangerous, indeed. Where water transportation depends upon muscles, the canoe has no equal. It is light and swift; it carries a good load; it walks the shallow waters; and it is easily portaged.

We continued down the Stikine to Wrangell; camping at Kloochman Canyon, near Little Canyon, at Barley Cache, and at Big Glacier. Near Wrangell, we passed a boat stranded on the shore. Though a new one, it was no-man's boat; for its owner, who was a prospector, had met his death a few days previously by drowning in the dangerous Stikine. The first flood will sweep the boat out to sea, equipped as its owner left it; for no one would take so much as a row lock, or a tow line, from such a boat.

These hunts are now a memory. Their real enchantment, the enchantment that endures, is not found in the slaying of a game animal; it is found in the many charms of nature revealed in the forests and the streams. That brilliant essayist, Richard Jefferies, personifies the wheat at harvest time, and causes the wheat to tell the little boy Guido of the happiness missed by many people. "If your people do not gather the flowers now, and watch the swallows, and listen to the blackbirds, whistling, as you are listening now while I talk, then Guido, my love, they will never pick any flowers, nor hear any birds' songs. They think they will, they think that when they have toiled, and worked for a long time, almost all their lives, then they will come to the flowers, and the birds, and be joyful in the sunshine. But no, it will not be so, for then they will be old themselves, and their ears dull, and their eyes dim, so that the birds will sound a great distance off, and the flowers will not seem bright." I take such trips as these that I may pick the flowers and hear the birds' songs; that I may enjoy nature as she came from the hand of God, untouched by the hand of man. And this I must do before my ears are dull or my eyes are dim. Sir Thomas Browne tells us that "art is the perfection of nature" and that "nature is the art of God" and that "though in a wilderness, a man is never alone." The mountains, the glaciers, the strong waters, the cascades, the birds and the beasts have taught me that this is so. "Heaven is under our feet as well as over our heads."

CHAPTER XII.

Wild Life and Sport in Bulgaria

By Henry W. Shoemaker,

American Minister, Sofia.

To one who truly loves the spirit of nature, it gives a great thrill to be in a country like Bulgaria, where there are wolves. Where wolves exist one can feel that primitive conditions have not yet been altogether destroyed, or nature's balance too greatly interfered with. The wolves of Bulgaria are probably the most interesting feature of the Continental fauna which is more nearly complete there than in any other country of Europe. At the present time the wolf (vulke) is found in all parts of Bulgaria, even on the plain surrounding the capital. Among the old mounted specimens at Sofia, in the Natural History Museum, one was killed in Tzar Ferdinand's Park, at Vrana, five miles from the heart of the city in 1907, another taken in 1900, is from the Baths at Banky, a popular outlying district, another taken in 1904 is from Negoven, also in the suburbs. Three wolves were killed at Pantcherevo, within five miles of Sofia, during the winter of 1930-1931.

Stories of their ferocity are many. During the winter of 1928-29 a soldier at Kniajevo, a popular resort, within five miles of the capital, was killed at his post and eaten by wolves.

During the World War, in the severe winter of 1917-1918, Lieut. Ivan Stancioff, now a second secretary in the Foreign Office at Sofia, was in command of a detachment of Marines on the Danube, near Roustchuk, and gave three of his men leave to visit at their homes in a nearby village. The men were overtaken by wolves in a snowstorm, eaten and nothing left of them but the soles of their shoes. A young engineer, working at the new waterworks for the city of Sofia in the Rila Mountains, during the winter of 1929-1930 was returning to camp with a peasant, when he was told by the latter to climb a tree as fast as he could. They were barely comfortably seated in the branches, when five wolves trotted by, "off the wind;" if the wolves had scented them, the peasant said, they would have surrounded the trees until their victims, overcome by cold, had dropped down and, like fruit, been eaten.

At the Monastery of Dragalevtzy, on Mount Vitosha, in full view of Sofia, wolves were frequently encountered during the World War, and at various times since numbers of young ones were captured and peddled by peasants on the streets of Sofia, one being purchased by the former American Minister, the Honorable Charles S. Wilson, who kept it as a pet in the Legation garden until it grew so large, that he decided it was best to send it to His Majesty's Zoo. There however it was quickly killed by the other wolfish inmates, which are old animals, having been there since the time of King Boris III's accession to the Bulgarian throne in 1918.

A young lady employed at the American Legation tells of attending a cabin-party with some of her friends, at Pantcherevo, on the Bistritza River, which rises on Vitosha, several years ago: during the evening the dogs set up a terrific barking, and they looked out of the window to see several wolves cross the lawn. Wolf skins are to be obtained in great numbers at the market in Sofia, and can be seen hanging in front of shops in most fair-sized Bulgarian towns. The finest skins seem to be found in the east, at the fur stores at Varna, on the Black Sea. In a small collection of wolf skins made by the writer, the dimensions of the four largest from tip to tip are 81, 80, 79 and 78 inches respectively.

Wolf hunting was practised as a sport by the household of former Tzar Ferdinand, who was an ardent sportsman as well as naturalist, and several fine wolves were shot on drives, about twenty years ago by General Pierre Markoff, the ex-Tzar's personal aide de camp, in the main chain of the Balkan Mountains, near Sofia. Wolf hunting in Bulgaria however is generally carried on by the members of the branches of the Hunters' Fraternity, which numbers over 35,000 members.

When wolves create havoc among the flocks at a village, the members of the Fraternity turn out, assisted by forest guards and the entire population. This general hunt is called a *hika*. The hunters take up positions on the paths where the wolves are likely to travel back to the mountains, while the villagers form a wide circle gradually closing in on the animals and driving them up to the guns.

Trapping is not practised, as there is always the danger of bears, dogs, and other animals getting in the traps.

Of late poisoning has been resorted to by forest guards to reduce the wolf population, but many regard this as poor sportmanship, as it is. According to the President of the Hunters' Fraternity, General P. Salabashoff, veteran of the war of liberation, and other Bulgarian wars, 500 wolves are killed annually in Bulgaria, which is certainly many more than are successfully reared. At such a rate in ten years the wolf will be a vanished animal, and one of the most picturesque forms of the wild life of the Balkans gone forever.

Will the peasants be any better off? A few more lambs may be raised, that is all. Are the tribesmen of Algeria any better off since Jules Gerard and his lieutenants exterminated the lions of North Africa? There is no record to show that they are any richer, or their flocks any larger, than in the old days.

Though scarce in many parts of Europe, wolves are still occasionally found in all European countries except the British Isles, Holland and Belgium. In Belgium they were still met with in the Ardennes up to 1895.

The continued presence of wolves in Bulgaria has been ascribed by some to their numbers being recruited each winter by new arrivals crossing the ice on the Danube from Transylvania and Russia. This is unlikely, as the wolf rarely travels more than in a radius of thirty miles from his den, being notoriously a home-loving creature. If any wolves cross on the ice they are single individuals seeking refuge in Bulgaria from dogs or hunters.

The coloration of the Bulgarian wolves would seem at first to indicate various types, as the peasant hunters speak of red wolves, yellow wolves and blue wolves. The best skins are a blend of the three colors, indicating that a wolf, when taken prime, has a variegated coat, which is long, smooth and silky; whereas those taken in summer have short, rough, stiffish hair.

Occasionally, wolves almost black have been taken in Bulgaria and snowwhite wolves are, in very rare instances, met with. A large white wolf suddenly appeared among a party of haymakers, seated eating their lunch, under the trees, near the village of Rachanitza, in June, 1916.

Mature Bulgarian wolves are robust and powerful and of the type of the last French wolf at the Jardin des Plantes, Paris, old "Jacques," which died in the fall of 1925, aged sixteen years. Bulgarian wolves are said to live from ten to twenty years, and to have as high as ten young in a litter but five is the general size of the family. Comparing a photograph of "Jacques" made shortly before his death with the largest dog-wolf in His Majesty's Zoo at Sofia, the Bulgarian wolf is no more strongly built than his congener born in the land of the Franks.

The bear (*metchka*) of Bulgaria is a magnificent animal, but it is rapidly approaching extermination. The peasants seem to dread bears more than wolves, and spare no effort to destroy them. Even during the long reign of Tzar Ferdinand, before the World War, they were decreasing so fast that His Majesty made every effort to have them protected by a decree from his Council of Ministers. Up to the present time the local prejudices continue so strong, that a motion to protect them was defeated in 1931, but by so

285

narrow a margin that King Boris is hopeful of having the closed season placed on them next year.

During 1930, a bear and a cub were killed near Bistritza, a village on the slopes of Mount Vitosha within view of the American College of Sofia. These bears, mounted, are now in the Museum of the Hunters' Fraternity at Sofia.

Bears are found high up in most of the mountain ranges of Bulgaria, in the main Balkan chain, in the Little Balkans (Sredna Gora), the Rila, Rhodope and Pirin Mountains and occasionally in Ossogova Planina, the southeast.

During the great forest fire in the Rila Mountains in 1929, set American-fashion by sparks from a logging engine, when sixteen thousand acres of original growth timber were destroyed, two bears rushed from the burning woods, in the direction of King Boris who was leading the army of fire-fighters. Forest guards quickly raised their carbines, but the King ordered them back, saying that the bears had likely lost their cubs in the fire, and had troubles enough.

As evidence of the deep seated prejudice that can exist against an animal, Tzar Ferdinand offered to reimburse the peasants double the value of every domestic animal destroyed by bears; scores of claims were filed, some of which His Majesty personally investigated; in many cases the cattle or sheep had died natural deaths; others were killed by wolves, while some had been destroyed by the peasants themselves to secure the rewards. This reminds one of conditions in sheep raising sections of our own western states, where every lamb which perishes of disease or exposure on the range is charged up to bears or other "predatory" creatures and Government hunters are requisitioned to kill the wrongly condemned beasts.

In Bulgaria bears are most often hunted by solitary trackers, who follow their traces to their dens in the mountains, where the killing usually takes place. Most of the tracking is done in the summer time, after rains, but they are also hunted in this manner in the spring and fall, when there are light "tracking snows." Some Turkish hunters made a specialty of locating the dens of bears during the breeding season, to capture the cubs alive to sell to Gipsy bear trainers. Usually the mother bear is killed before the cubs can be secured.

Using traps to take bears is forbidden in Bulgaria, and the native hunters would scorn such a method as unsportsmanlike. Adult bears in Bulgaria sometimes weigh as high as 700 pounds, and 600 pound bears are not uncommon.

A party of Gipsies whose winter quarters is near the Greek frontier, have ten bears, the largest of which standing erect measures eight feet and its estimated weight is close to 700 pounds. A superb bear, standing erect, owned by an aged Gipsy at Tirnovo, an ancient capital of Bulgaria, measured by the writer last summer (1930), stood exactly seven feet six and three-quarter inches.

One of the favorite hunting stories of the Honorable Athanase Bouroff, Minister for Foreign Affairs of Bulgaria, and an ardent hunter and fly fisherman, is of an old Turk in the Stara Planina (the Bulgarian name for the Main Balkan Chain) who has been a lone tracker of bears for fifty years, having recently brought to Karlovo his sixty-fifth bear. Whenever a peasant reports a loss among his flocks the aged Turk goes in pursuit and tracks the alleged marauder into the most inaccessible mountain recesses, never returning to civilization until he has brought down the object of his chase. In wild state the coats of Bulgarian bears are of a decidedly chocolate brown color, some with much black underhair giving at a distance, an impression of blackness. The bears in the King's Zoo at Sofia, while not so dark as the wild ones, are far removed in color from the pasty, yellow, short-haired look of the bears led about by the Gipsies. Food and conditions of life evidently have much to do with their coloration.

Along the Black Sea coast the Jackal (Chaca) is found in fairly large numbers. They congregate in rocky places on the great dry plains back of the coast and yell in chorus like the coyotes of our western states. Summer tourists at Varna, the popular Bulgarian Black Sea resort, drive in the evenings to the village of Peynardjik, to hear the jackals' music. The jackals at present seem to have a tendency to extend their range westward, as the writer has seen a skin of a jackal killed at Yundullah in 1930, almost in the centre of Bulgaria, although until recently they were found only on the Dalmatian Coast. However they seem to be most plentiful along the Black Sea coast in Bulgaria, from the Danube Delta to the Turkish border. A very fine jackal from Peynardjik was captured alive in May, 1931, and presented to the King.

Wildcats (*Felis catus*), exist everywhere in Bulgaria where there are large forests. They are found close to Sofia on the Vitosha. They exist in one race, but two shades of skin, a lighter and a darker, but the cause of this difference in pelage is unknown.

The writer has skins of both types in his collection. At least a hundred wild-cat skins are brought every winter to the Sofia market and half as many to Varna. The rare European lynx (*Ris*), which is protected, is said to exist in the Strandja Mountains, near the Turkish border, in southeastern Bulgaria. It may be of *L. pardina variety*. Formerly its range was in most of the forested parts of Bulgaria, the last one having been killed at Temir Kapia, near Samokof, thirty miles from Sofia, in 1905. The writer saw a lynx skin in the Sofia market in October, 1930, but was unable to learn where it had been taken. The lynx is said to be still fairly plentiful north of the Danube in Transylvania.

The fox (*Lissitza*) which exists all over Bulgaria, is of a large variety. The majority of them are red, but occasionally black skins are received in the Sofia market. One cross-fox skin, extremely rare for Bulgaria, came to the Sofia market in April, 1931.

Martens, weasels, otters, badgers and other valuable furbearers are also fairly abundant, and some fine skins frequently appear at the Sofia market. Large hares abound and many can be seen on the roads during a motor trip at night.

Along the Black Sea coast a large variety of seal (*Pelagus monachus*) is still found. His Majesty King Boris III with Dr. Ivan Bouresch, Director of the Royal Natural History Collections at Sofia, observed one swimming in the Black Sea off the Palace of Euxinograd, near Varna, in March, 1923. Their rookeries exist near Kaliakra, close to the Roumanian frontier, and at Zectin Bouroum, near Bourgas, much further south. Tzar Ferdinand placed a closed season on the seals prior to 1914.

When one comes to the subject of the game animals

of Bulgaria, the first to be mentioned is the red deer, said to be the purest race of *Cervus elephus* in Europe. These superb animals have become very rare, and despite a closed season since 1907, poachers are still further reducing their numbers. Prior to the liberation from the Turks, in 1878, the red deer were found in large herds on the grassy slopes of Balkans, fifteen to twenty miles north-east of Sofia. According to General Markoff, the more prosperous Turks did very little hunting except falconry, and most of the Bulgarians in those days were not allowed to carry fire-arms. Had it not been for Tzar Ferdinand's zealous interest, from the time of his accession to the throne in 1887, wild life in Bulgaria would now be a thing of the past, as, rejoicing in the free possession of arms, every man aims to be a killer of game.

The stag was usually hunted by stalking in the Scottish method. At present the red deer are found in the Strandja Planina, near Bourgas, where King Boris and Dr. Bouresch came upon a herd of six in the spring of 1931, in the Kodja Balkan, further north near Varna, and a few in the central part of the Stara Planina, near Kalofer on the slopes of Peak Ferdinand, the highest mountain in the Balkan range.

Next in importance as a game animal in Bulgaria is the chamois, which has been given protection for five years, from 1931, owing to inroads made by illegal hunting.

The chamois is still found in the Rila Mountains of Central Bulgaria, above an altitude of 6500 feet, but in severe winters they are found as low as 4500 feet.

In the western Rhodopes they are found eastward to Belmeken, Suitkaia, Karlik and Tchepelar. In the main Balkan Mountains of Central Bulgaria, in the vicinity of Kalofer they were most numerous, and for that reason hardest hunted.

One old Turkish cobbler who has his shop near the gates of one of the Mosques at the beautiful mountain town of Karlovo, where he is also "sexton," was for many years an inveterate chamois hunter. He would disappear from his bench every few months, go alone to the highest crags of Peak Ferdinand, invariably returning with a chamois on his shoulders. In his solitary hunting he had killed over two hundred chamois up to the time the five year closed season went into effect.

Third in importance as a game animal in Bulgaria is the roebuck which like the deer and the chamois have become rarer recently from excessive hunting with dogs. They are now protected for a five year season, beginning 1931.

Roebucks are found all over the wooded portions of the country, but according to Foreign Minister Bouroff, are now most numerous in the virgin oak forests near the Black Sea, in southeastern Bulgaria. They are still found occasionally within sight of Sofia on Mount Vitosha and in the Lulin Mountains, behind the Sofia aviation field at Bojouritche.

Fourth in importance as a game animal in Bulgaria is the wild boar. It was also "sport royal" of His Majesty until recently when, because of their growing scarcity, he abandoned their chase, to set an example. These formidable beasts attain immense proportions in Bulgaria, and exist in all parts of the country where there are woods, but are most plentiful in the Rila Mountains, and in the Rhodopes in the region of the scrub pine (*Pinus montanus*). They are abundant around the King's Hunting Lodge at Tcham-Koria, thirty-five miles from Sofia, but the last on Mount Vitosha, on the outskirts of Sofia was killed a few years ago. During the World War they appeared in the Boris Park within the city limits. Owing to their destruction of the peasants' crops and early vegetables, they are afforded no protection in Bulgaria. The peasant hunters penetrate the dense thickets where the wild boars harbor, and with dogs drive them down to the open pastures at the foot of the mountains, where members of the Hunters' Fraternity are lined up to shoot them.

Among the birds of Bulgaria there is an almost un-broken European avifauna.

The Lammergeier (*Bradat orel*), greatest of Con-tinental birds of prey, was given perpetual protection by Tzar Ferdinand in 1896. They are rigorously pre-served and from the best information there are now about twenty breeding pairs still existing in the wilder parts of the Rila Mountains, near Karlik in the Rhodopes, and on the inaccessible heights of the Stara Planina, or Main Balkan Mountain, especially on the Peak Ferdinand near Kalofer.

A pair of lammergeiers have bred regularly every season in the King's Zoological garden in Sofia, since 1916. Two eggs are laid, the period of incubation being 54 days; after the tenth day the mother bird kills the weaker of the two youngsters and feeds it to the strongest. The King for several years had the weaker nestlings removed, but no efforts could keep them from dying; he then decided to let the relent-less instinct of the ages, caused most likely by food scarcity in a wild state, take its course. In 1931 the young were hatched on March 15th; in 1930 on March 5th. There are now eleven specimens of these magnificent birds in His Majesty's Zoo.

At the present time the lammergeier is entirely extinct in Europe except for a few in the Pyrenees and in Sardinia, at which latter place they have been given protection by another great ruler and ornithologist Benito Juares Mussolini.

Shortly after Tzar Ferdinand came to Bulgaria, in 1887, a huge lammergeier rested on a chimney pot in Sofia. A sweep struck it down with his broom handle, injuring a wing.

His Majesty heard of it, and had it sent to his newly-formed Zoo, where it lived only six months. It is now mounted in the Palace at Varna, and has the yellow coloration on the neck, which specimens long in captivity always lose. It was due to this bird that Tzar Ferdinand became especially interested in the protection of the species in Bulgaria.

The golden or "royal" eagle (*Aquila chrysaetus*) and the imperial eagle (*Aquila imperialis*) are found throughout Bulgaria, and in such numbers that no protection is afforded them. The sea eagle (*Haliaetus leucoryphus*) is a resident of the Black Sea coast, where a noble specimen, now in His Majesty's Zoo, was found with its talons frozen in the ice, and secured by Lieut. Stancioff's servants.

A specimen of the rare Egyptian eagle was killed in the Rose Valley in Central Bulgaria, by General Salabashoff in 1928. Hawks and falcons of all kinds abound.

The Eagle-Owl (*Bouhal*) or "Grand Duke" is plentiful, and is not given protection.

Of game birds an interesting feature of Bulgaria is that the European pheasant (*Phasianus colchicus*) exists in a wild state only in Bulgaria; they are most plentiful in the oak forests near Bourgas and in the vicinity of Yambol. They have no white "collar" like the pheasants descended from the Asiatic types, commonly known as "ring necks" in the United States and elsewhere.

Perhaps the grandest game bird in Bulgaria is the Auerhahn (*Tetrao urogallus*) of which King Boris considers the Bulgarian specimens as being on an average of smaller size and weight than those in Tcheco-Slovakia. This difference is easily noted in comparing mounted specimens. At present these are the only game hunted by His Majesty, as his efforts are largely to conserve the wild life of Bulgaria, and in the spring of 1931 he had a "record" bag of five. The flesh of the Auerhahn when prepared in the German style makes very delicious eating. The Auerhahn, called in the British Isles capercailzie, is found only in pine and beech woods in Bulgaria. It exists now in the following localities: the main chain of the Balkans, from near Berkovitza in the west, eastward to Mourgash and in the vicinity of the famous Shipka Pass; on the entire massif of the Rila (the Sofia watershed); the entire range of the Rhodopes. In parts of the Pirin Mountains, around Ali-Barouch — near the Greek

frontier it is said to occur. Those who hunt the Auerhahn regularly claim that about 500 of these grand
birds remain in Bulgaria.

Hunting the Auerhahn is arduous though thrilling
sport and one of the best descriptions of the way it is
done in the Continental method before daybreak, is
contained in A. Baillie-Grohmann's excellent work
Sport in the Alps.

Next in importance as a game bird in Bulgaria is
the great bustard (*Otis tarda*), called in Bulgaria the
"Dropla" and "wild turkey". This splendid bird is a
migrant to the vast agricultural plains, after the wheat
is harvested in the fall when it appears on the dry
stubblefields. Being a visitor only, it is not protected,
yet, though frequently met with, few are killed. Unfortunately the stalking horse has given way to the
"flivver" and the bustard is now hunted in Bulgaria
by alleged sportsmen in automobiles; likewise in
Spain it is said that this rare bird is hunted in air-
planes. It is most frequently seen on the plains in the
north-eastern parts of Bulgaria, in the districts of
Varna, Rousse and Razgrade, though it occasionally
appears on the plains of Sofia, almost to the edge of
Boris Park, and in the prairie country about Philippopolis in south-central Bulgaria.

When in 1887 Tzar Ferdinand located his first
country estate at Kritchim, near Philippopolis, he was

led to do so by the park-like groves of primeval oaks which adorned the level terrain and also by the fact that many bustards made it a favorite resting place during their migrations. Some of these birds still return to ornament this royal estate and present a striking picture walking proudly about under the giant trees. To this park Tzar Ferdinand brought also a number of fallow deer from Austria, some of which have been liberated in the nearby Rhodopes Mountains.

The little bustard or Strepet, also called the Houbara, also exists on the vast plains of Bulgaria and is more frequently met with than the great bustard. This writer has one in his collection which was taken by a professional bird-stuffer in 1930, near Kazanlik, in the Rose Valley.

Quails appear in the spring, and their incessant chirping is a familiar sound in the growing wheat. After the harvest they congregate in vast numbers preparatory to their southerly flights. In the late summer of 1930, quails rose by the tens of thousands in front of the writer's automobile on the waterless, thistle-covered plains, south of the Bulgarian border in Greece, on the road to Salonika. It was the most impressive spectacle of game birds he had ever seen.

Great flocks of white ibises were also seen in the

newly ploughed fields on the edge of this vast "desert."

Partridges are very abundant, as are woodcocks, snipe, and all varieties of water fowl. There is much professional duck hunting on the Danube, and on inlets of the Black Sea, to supply the Sofia market.

That game is as plentiful as it is in Bulgaria, and that there have been so few species exterminated in the last half century, is due entirely to the zealous efforts of two naturalist sovereigns, former Tzar Ferdinand and his son, the present king, Boris. They strove to create a sentiment favorable to wild life, and in the main have succeeded. When one considers that Bulgaria is smaller than Pennsylvania, and has a population nearly as large, it is remarkable that it is still a hunter's delight and above all a naturalist's laboratory.

Falconry, up to the time of the liberation 1877-78, was the favorite sport of the ruling class of Turks in Bulgaria. Certain villages were famous as training places for hawks, and some Bulgarian hawk-trainers enjoyed a wide celebrity throughout the Near East. Most of the hawking was done on the open plains, where the hawks were flown at bustards, hares and partridges, and, near the water courses, at cranes, herons and other water birds. With the departure of most of the Turkish officials and landowners, falconry

rapidly fell into disuse, although the old time fal-
coners love to tell of the days when it was the royal
sport of the country.

The Bulgarian game laws, modelled largely on
those of pre-war Austria and Germany, would be
more effective if market hunting was eliminated. By
professional hunters scouring the woods all kinds of
wild life are destroyed as "pot shots," and on the
chance that the skins often can be sold to collectors.
Exhibitions of mounted wild animals and birds are
held in Sofia, where the birdstuffers dispose of their
specimens. On the other hand the village life of Bulgaria leaves vast uninhabited areas for the birds and
the game, and the forests and open plains are not
dotted with farms or cabins as in the United States,
so there are natural "sanctuaries" for wild life to exist
practically unmolested.

Hunters have to travel long distances to the game
fields and no one lives permanently in the haunts of
wild life, except forest guards or road-menders.

Many members of the diplomatic corps in Sofia are
ardent hunters, but are interested mostly in water
fowl, partridge and quail shooting, which may be
obtained in the Sofia plain and nearby marshlands. A
few venture further afield, into the mountains in
pursuit of the auerhahn.

The trout streams of Bulgaria are pure, and well

stocked, although fishing for market has depleted many of the brooks nearer to Sofia. Mr. Bouroff, the Foreign Minister, is an enthusiastic fly fisherman, and in his leisure hours travels all over Bulgaria to enjoy his favorite sport. He often brings diplomats with him as his guests, and as he knows the best streams, these outings are thoroughly enjoyed by those fortunate enough to participate in them.

This chapter has not attempted to describe the song birds of Bulgaria. There are many varieties, of which the most noticeable, and one of the most plentiful is the nightingale, which sings every evening in the Boris Park, Sofia, from the first part of May until the latter part of June, nor can it tell of the multitudes of brightly plumaged, insectivorous birds which fill the forests with their voices and busy activity. The green jays, the green rollers, the hoopoes, and magpies are the familiar roadside birds of Bulgaria. No mention has been made of the vast numbers of storks which nest on chimneys and feed on the plains in company with large grey herons, watching the watercourses in the rice fields. Suddenly, generally on August 15th, the storks from every locality gather together in open fields, and joining flocks of hundreds of thousands of their kind, start for their winter sojourn in Africa.

The varied wild life of Bulgaria makes a stay in

the country an unending delight, and a series of surprizes, and no one could feel boredom or ennui where wolf and bear stories abound, and there are bird songs and flights of birds.

As proof that the balance of nature is undisturbed in Bulgaria, there is probably no country in Europe where there are more eagles, hawks, crows, ravens and owls, yet song birds and game birds exist in abundance. In fact there are said to be more nightingales in Bulgaria than in any other European country. It is only when man has destroyed song birds and game birds that one begins to hear of "predatory" birds; they have long been the smoke screen to excuse man's relentless slaughter of the song and game birds, in most of Europe and in the United States.

Even beyond the interest created by a love of wild nature and sport, is the store of animal and bird folklore. Every wild beast and bird has its cycle of quaint tales, while vampire stories give a gruesome background to all fireside legends.

Any country which exterminates its wild life, no matter for what reasons, will pay a heavy penalty in spiritual death in the minds of old and young alike.

It is the life of the field and the forest which keeps mankind eternally young. There can be no enervation or decadence in a land where the sport of the chase exists. End it, and the apathy and decay of urban civilization quickly follows.